GUERRILLA ADVERTISING 2

GUERRILLA ADVERTISING 2
MORE UNCONVENTIONAL BRAND
COMMUNICATION

GAVIN LUCAS

LAURENCE KING PUBLISHING

LAURENCE KING

Published in 2011 by
Laurence King Publishing Ltd
361–373 City Road
London EC1V 1LR
United Kingdom

Tel: + 44 20 7841 6900
Fax: + 44 20 7841 6910
E-mail: enquiries@laurenceking.com
www.laurenceking.com

A catalogue record for this book is available
from the British Library.

ISBN: 978-1-85669-747-7

Design: Intercity
www.intercitystudio.com

Editorial Director: Jo Lightfoot

Printed in China

CONTENTS

INTRODUCTION

> Whosoever desires
> constant success must
> change his conduct
> with the times.

NICCOLÒ MACHIAVELLI, THE PRINCE, 1513

Advancing technology provides us with ever more sophisticated and complex ways of communicating, accessing and sharing information. It is hard to believe that just five years ago, when *Guerrilla Advertising* was published, most of us had never heard of Facebook or Twitter – and Apple had yet to unleash its first mobile phone, the iPhone. It is also hard to conceive now that in another five years, Facebook, Twitter and the iPhone and iPad may well be replaced by new technologies and concepts that will seem more relevant or pertinent to the way we live our lives. C'est la vie.

As with the first volume, the aim of *Guerrilla Advertising 2* is to showcase campaigns from around the world, all of which engage the public in ways that are remarkable for their originality, using means and methods that are strikingly appropriate to the product or service being promoted.

Did you see the hot-air balloon that was dressed to look just like the house buoyed by balloons in the Disney/Pixar film, *Up*, as it flew over Europe to promote the film's DVD launch? Were you there when a flash-mob of dancers performed a routine at a packed Liverpool Street train station in a T-Mobile promotion? Perhaps you found a circular sticker stuck to the sole of your shoe, which, on closer inspection, warned of the horrors of landmines. Or maybe you were impressed by AC/DC's video, delivered to fans by Sony's inventive digital department as animated text embedded in an Excel spreadsheet. Maybe you didn't witness these things but heard about them from a friend who did, read about them on a blog or saw them on the news. All these events and activities are evidence of the variety of methods which brands and their agencies are employing to get their messages across.

The continuing challenge for brands and advertisers is that established, obvious forms of advertising simply become background noise in the busy lives of today's consumers. 'If we continue to define ourselves as an industry as being in "advertising", my belief is we're pretty much doomed,' wrote Ty Montague for the foreword of the original *Guerrilla Advertising* book, when he was co-president and chief creative officer at JWT New York. 'The advertising business – the business of interrupting what people are interested in with a commercial message about something they're not interested in – is a business that is already in decline,' he continued. 'The good news: there is a new business being born simultaneously, literally all around us. Call it engagement, interactivity, participation ... The fact is that it doesn't really have a satisfactory name yet. That will probably come later. But it is being born ...

Small groups of people, working in isolation from one another and often employing untested new technologies are creating new ways of telling stories.'

Montague's prediction that traditional advertising agencies must reject old formulas in favour of investigating new methods of brand communication has come to pass – although there is no sign of the industry adopting a new name for what it now offers. Rather, the definition of the word advertising has changed. It has become a blanket term which covers the different approaches to brand communication that these agencies now have to consider: PR, guerrilla, experiential, ambient, TV, press, digital, behavioural and integrated – or 360 degree – marketing.

Currently there are a huge number of media options available for advertisers to consider when planning a campaign strategy. Yet it seems futile to list them here. Why? Because – and please forgive the cliché – the advertising industry is in a state of flux. This isn't a phase it's going through. In all probability, it will forever be in flux because technology is constantly reshaping the media landscape at such a rate that it's now impossible for the ad industry to settle on a formula for creating advertising in the way that it did in the latter half of the twentieth century, when the 30-second TV spot was king. It's not just impossible to come up with a new advertising formula – it is now completely inappropriate.

Even television itself has changed, and long gone are the days when a handful of channels each promised massive viewing figures for advertisers. Watching TV used to be a passive activity, but more and more it is an active one, with viewers subscribing to digital television services now having the option of pausing, fast-forwarding and rewinding programmes as they wish. Online media stores such as Apple's iTunes, along with internet TV services such as BBC iPlayer and video sharing websites YouTube and Vimeo, offer their users the opportunity to watch whatever they want, whenever they want. Add to this the arrival of the iPhone and other smart phones with their big, high-resolution screens, built-in cameras and fast internet access. These hand-held gadgets allow us to watch TV, send and receive emails, investigate and forward links to content that is engaging enough to warrant our interest, and create and share our own content – wherever we might be.

Consumers can also use their pocket-sized computers to buy products online. And brands have realized that they can offer services through these devices – brand communications that are actually useful to consumers and relevant for that particular gadget. Hundreds of thousands of applications, or apps, for the iPhone are downloaded every week from Apple's app store. These apps could be games, or handy tools that make use of the iPhone's functionality – its touchscreen, accelerometer, camera, or built-in GPS. The device and the larger, more recently launched iPad, are interesting new additions to the media advertisers can explore. London agency Brothers and Sisters, for example, created a clever iPhone app that made use of Google Maps and geotagging technology to link historical images of London scenes from the Museum of London's art and photographic collections to the locations they actually depict on the map (see pages 90–95). Not only that, but users in one of the featured locations can click the '3D View' button and the app will recognize the user's location and overlay the historical image on the view through the iPhone's camera lens. Rather than simply telling consumers about their client, with this campaign agency Brothers and Sisters successfully created an engaging way to use the technology in people's pockets to allow them to interact and explore the image collection of the Museum of London.

Consumers now play a crucial role in the distribution of brand messages. It is up to them to get involved and pass the message on, either digitally or physically. The Japanese edition of *Guerrilla Advertising* (see pages 26–27) sported a hardback cover that extended beyond the pages of the book and featured cut-out carrier bag-style handles. This allowed the book to be carried around, rather like a shopping bag, meaning the book itself became the medium for a clever guerrilla campaign that would appeal to the very people who might buy it.

This is not to say that TV advertising (or mass media advertising, for that matter) is dead. Nothing could be further from the truth. On one hand, there are still media slots to be bought during huge TV events, such as international sporting fixtures, that will be viewed by millions. On the other hand, more specialized television channels mean that advertisers have a chance to communicate directly to target audiences. Digital television also offers new opportunities to advertisers. A seemingly traditional ad could prompt users to explore interactive content by pressing the red button on their remote controls.

TV advertising, although still a hugely expensive undertaking, is now just one of innumerable tools in the box of media options that can be combined in a process of integrated brand promotion. This approach to brand communication might make use of any number of media channels, conspiring to communicate an over-arching idea, in order to

effectively engage consumers. A good example of this kind of approach is Saatchi & Saatchi's Dance campaign for T-Mobile (see pages 178–179). On the morning of January 15, 2009, dozens of dancers, dressed to blend in with the hundreds of commuters passing through London's Liverpool Street train station, performed a lively routine to a medley of feel-good dancefloor classics, played over the station's intercom system while hidden cameras filmed the activity – which included the spontaneous reaction of the commuters among whom the action took place. Within 48 hours, a three-minute film of it was aired on TV, filling an entire commercial break during *Celebrity Big Brother* on Channel 4. After the TV premiere, a shorter, 60-second version ran for two weeks, followed by ads that included specific product and price plan information. Viewers of the ad were encouraged to press the red button on their remote to view extra footage of the making of the advert.

In tandem with this activity, T-Mobile also created a dedicated YouTube channel where users could upload their own videos and view films of celebrities being taught how to do the T-Mobile dance by choreographer Bryony Albert. All of the campaign's various iterations supported T-Mobile's advertising strapline: 'Life's for sharing' – the idea being that as a network, T-Mobile lets its customers share with each other the things in life worth sharing, which, presumably, includes a seemingly spontaneous outbreak of synchronized dancing in a train station at rush hour. Bizarre, perhaps, but it paid off. At the time of writing, the three-minute version of the film has been watched on YouTube nearly 24.5 million times.

Increasingly, as this campaign demonstrates rather well, brand communication is less about sending out messages, and more about engagement and social interaction. Brands want to nurture communities of loyal consumers. And to do that effectively, they need to understand their audience. Consumer insight is a must when conceiving any brand campaign in the twenty-first century. If you misunderstand your audience's wants, needs and expectations, how can you hold their attention, earn their respect and, ultimately, persuade them to invest in what you have to offer?

Of course, funding an advertising campaign can be an expensive business. At the time of writing, the world is still recovering from the global recession that began in late 2007. We also live in a time when many companies like to have green credentials and be ethically sound in principle and practice. Anyone with an internet connection can look up information about a company so businesses have to operate in a way that reflects this. Advertising agencies have to offer more than good ideas and solutions to brands' communication problems – they have to offer value for money and practise what they preach, now more than ever. And paying clients have never wanted more bang for their buck. Brands don't just want us to simply see their adverts anymore. They want us to engage with, respond to, photograph, talk and blog about them.

Mass media approaches to brand communications, while ever more tricky to orchestrate, will never be redundant. In this book there are several campaigns that, while implemented in specific locations – themselves chosen because of the sheer volume of people passing through daily – were designed to be impressive or engaging enough to attract the attention of the press and thus reach an even wider audience. For example, TBWA\Berlin's Impossible Huddle campaign for adidas (featured on pages 154–155),

consisted of giant sculptures of eleven top European football players (all sponsored by adidas, naturally) placed in the main concourse of Zurich's Central Station for the duration of the UEFA EURO 2008 soccer tournament. The Swiss rail authority reported than an estimated 13 million people passed through the station during the three-week period, and the enormous installation was impossible to miss. As well as this, various news titles such as the BBC, *Financial Times*, *Die Welt*, *Gazetta dello Sport*, *Le Parisien* and *NRC Handelsblad* featured the campaign on their front pages or online editions – and it was picked up by dozens if not hundreds of blogs worldwide.

So, it is clear that advertising is no longer confined to TV ad breaks and poster sites, and never will be again. As many of the campaigns gathered in this book attest, there is no surface or space that brands will not utilize or fill with their communication strategies – both online, and offline in the real world.

But as we move forward in an increasingly media- and internet-savvy world, brand campaigns will have to be clever and pitched perfectly in order to impress and engage their intended audiences. Otherwise, we the public will use those same places and spaces to ridicule their efforts, rather than applaud them.

STREET PROPAG-ANDA

EXECUTIVE CREATIVE
DIRECTORS
DAVID GUERRERO, JOEL
LIMCHOC, SIMON WELSH

CREATIVE DIRECTORS
BRANDIE TAN,
TIN SANCHEZ

ART DIRECTOR
GARY AMANTE

COPYWRITER
REY TIEMPO

PHOTOGRAPHER
MARLON BALANGON

PRINT PRODUCER
AL SALVADOR

COMPUTER ARTIST
MANNY VAILOCES

ACCOUNTS
OMBET TRASPE,
SHIRLEY GADIA

TITLE
BIKE CLOCK

CLIENT
PIZZA HUT

AGENCY
BBDO GUERRERO / PROXIMITY PHILIPPINES

Pizza-delivery bikes were deemed the perfect medium to deliver not only pizzas but a brand message for Pizza Hut in this campaign devised by Philippines-based agency BBDO Guerrero/Proximity Philippines.

Large digital clock displays, which counted down from the maximum promised time for delivery, were placed on selected pizza-delivery bikes – thus showing all and sundry the restaurant chain's commitment to its policy of 'hot and on time or your pizza's free'.

TITLE
BIG BUSH

CLIENT
STRIP.COM.SG

AGENCY
JWT SINGAPORE

Enormous knickers placed strategically on bushes was the simple but amusing idea conjured up by JWT Singapore to promote the body-hair removal services of Strip.com.sg.

EXECUTIVE CREATIVE
DIRECTORS
**ALI SHABAZ,
TAY GUAN HIN**

ART DIRECTOR
THOMAS YANG

COPYWRITERS
**JOSEPH CHEONG,
ANDREW MCKECHNIE**

TITLE
DONKEY KONG SCAFFOLD
CLIENT
**COMPUTERSPIELE
MUSEUM BERLIN**
AGENCY
**SCHOLZ & FRIENDS,
BERLIN**

In December 2006, agency Scholz & Friends turned a scaffold-clad apartment block in Berlin into a huge advertisement for the city's Computer Game Museum. By laying printed canvas covers of various graphic elements from the original Donkey Kong platform game over the scaffold, they made it look like it was a huge screen from the game.

During the month the installation was live website traffic to computerspielemuseum.de increased by 38% above the average monthly hit rate.

CREATIVE DIRECTORS
**MATTHIAS SPAETGENS,
JAN LEUBE**

ART DIRECTOR
CARLO JOEST

COPYWRITER
FOLKE RENKEN

PHOTOGRAPHER
TOBIAS KRUSE

AGENCY PRODUCER
SOEREN GESSAT

ACCOUNT MANAGERS
**KATRIN SEEGERS, ANNE
LADEGAST, SVEN WEICHE,
LAURA AUERSWALD**

TITLE
DROOLING DOG

CLIENT
ROYAL CANIN

AGENCY
HEYE & PARTNER

This amusing campaign saw Hamburg agency Heye & Partner book two billboards that faced each other across a pedestrian walkway. One billboard ran a packshot of Royal Canin dog food, while the facing billboard had a portrait shot of a Great Dane that appeared to be looking longingly at the dog food pictured directly opposite. Furthermore, drool from the dog's mouth dribbled down the billboard, creating a puddle on the pavement beneath.

Apparently, the drool was made with water and jam sugar and was secreted by a specially devised canister and tube hidden behind the billboard.

CREATIVE DIRECTOR
KARSTEN KUHN

COPYWRITER
JOST KAEHLER

ART DIRECTORS
LINDA TIEMANN,
JULIA HELLWEGE

MANAGING DIRECTOR
DETLEF ARNOLD

PHOTOGRAPHERS
HOLGER KIRK (DOG);
THOMAS SCHMITZ
(PACKSHOT)

MEDIA BOOKING
OMG OUTDOOR GMBH,
HAMBURG

PRINTING
STAUDIGL-DRUCK GMBH
& CO. KG, DONAUWÖRTH

PLACARDING
AWK AUSSENWERBUNG
GMBH, HAMBURG

AGENCY PRODUCER
CORINNA BONSEN

ACCOUNT MANAGER
DANIEL BREMER

ACCOUNT EXECUTIVE
JANA KRUSE

IMAGE EDITING
MAX HORNÄK

INSTALLATION
ANDRÉ MARTENS

TITLE
SUMMER MADNESS
CLIENT
FROSTY FRUITS
AGENCY
PUBLICIS MOJO, MELBOURNE

To promote Nestlé Peters Ice Cream Frosty Fruits fruit ice, agency Publicis Mojo, Melbourne, erected a series of eye-catching, colourful statues of Summer Madness victims – people who had failed to stay cool in the heat of the summer – in Sydney and Melbourne. Each of the 4-m (13-ft) tall statues was installed on a stone plinth and was accompanied by an explanatory plaque.

The models for the statues were created in the UK (in Hackney, east London) by the artist and model maker Wilfrid Wood, who is represented by agency Dutch Uncle.

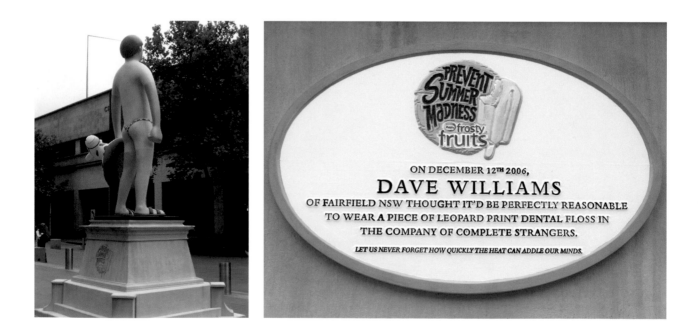

CREATIVE DIRECTOR
LEON WILSON

CREATIVES
LEA EGAN, JONTY BELL

CHARACTER DESIGN
WILFRID WOOD

SCULPTOR
JOSH YOUNG

AGENCY PRODUCER
TREVOR HUNTER

PROJECT MANAGER
RACHAEL SCHEFFER

On January 23rd 2003, Lana Bradford of Brighton VIC braided her hair, rented some skates, and threw away her dignity. Let us never forget how quickly the heat can addle our minds.

TITLE
**GUERRILLA ADVERTISING,
JAPANESE EDITION**

AGENCY
TOKYU AGENCY INC.

CREATIVE DESIGNER
RYOKO NAGAMATSU

PHOTOGRAPHER
DAISUKE YAMASHITA

Since the English version is also available in Japan, I wanted the Japanese version to maintain the same colour, typeface and cover design. I wanted everyone to instantly recognize this as the Japanese version of the English book. I also hope that people will carry this around using the handles and consequently advertise the book.

RYOKO NAGAMATSU

When Tokyu Agency's publishing department decided to publish a Japanese-language edition of *Guerrilla Advertising*, they gave the book's bright yellow cover a design tweak to maximize its visual impact. Ryoko Nagamatsu, the creative designer, came up with the idea of a bag-like book that people could carry around. The cover was hardback, with the front and back covers extended beyond the pages of the book to incorporate cut-out carrier bag-style handles. The agency photographed people of all ages and walks of life carrying the book around in fashionable parts of Tokyo, such as Ginza, Aoyama and Shibuya – thus creating a guerrilla-style campaign for the book itself. The pictures (some of which are shown here) appeared on the inside front and back covers of the Japanese version.

TITLE
SCRATCHES ON YOUR CAR
CLIENT
VRIJVERZEKERD.NL
AGENCY
NOVOCORTEX

Imagine the feeling. You're just returning to your car after a spot of shopping, and as you approach you can see that your car's got a big set of fresh scratches on the rear door. Your heart starts racing. Some idiot has scraped your car. Badly. However, as you get closer, the scratches start looking less like scratches ... and words are discernible among the black marks you thought were scratches: 'Repairing your damages can be as easy as removing this sticker. Insure your car on VrijVerzekerd.nl.'

Yes, charged with the task of building brand awareness for Dutch online car insurance company VrijVerzekerd, creative agency Novocortex printed the scratches on hundreds of easily removed static cling stickers, which also bore the above message.

After placing dozens of the stickers on cars in Amsterdam, the agency secretly filmed reactions of car owners using hidden cameras, uploaded a video of clips to YouTube and sent a link to marketing blogs. As well as posting the video, the agency invited blog readers to take some stickers and have fun with their colleagues and friends.

The video was viewed around 10,000 times within a month of going online – and it achieved #29 in the YouTube ranking for the Most Viewed Humorous Videos in the Netherlands. At the time of writing, the video has notched up around 50,000 views and a follow-up campaign film has been viewed approximately 15,000 times. The invitation to test stickers on friends and family was published by about 20 blogs and online communities in the Netherlands and Belgium. 'We ran out of stickers in two days,' says the agency. 'Most of the stickers were spread by blog readers and the daily traffic on vrijverzekerd.nl tripled, while time spent on the site increased by 20%.'

STRATEGY DIRECTOR
SERGE FENENKO

CREATIVE DIRECTORS
**NADIA ZELENKOVA,
ILYA ANDREYEV**

ART DIRECTOR
IRA ZNOSOK

CLIENT CONTACT
IET JONGBLOED

CREATIVE DIRECTORS
TONY GRANGER, KERRY
KEENAN, ALISON
GRAGNANO

ART DIRECTORS
MICHAEL SCHACHTNER,
MENNO KLUIN

COPYWRITER
JULIA NEUMANN

AGENCY PRODUCERS
ZAMILE VILAKAZI, GERRY
BOYLE, ALLI TAYLOR,
DEAN SHOUKAS

GIANT INFLATABLE
SPECIALIST
PUBLI AIR

PRODUCTION COMPANY
SOFT CITIZEN

TITLE
GLIDE PIG
CLIENT
GLIDE DENTAL FLOSS
AGENCY
SAATCHI & SAATCHI,
NEW YORK

To advertise Glide dental floss – a product capable of removing any wedged foodstuffs from between teeth – Saatchi & Saatchi created this enormous inflatable pig and had it wedged between two buildings in Toronto in this hugely original and eye-catching campaign.

TITLE
GLOBAL DOWNTURN
CLIENT
FINANCIAL TIMES
AGENCY
DDB LONDON

These clever ads for the *Financial Times* question the wisdom of cutting advertising budgets at a time of economic downturn. A selection of billboard sites were stripped bare and a small panel of copy was placed top right that reads: 'Global downturn. What's the first mistake businesses make?'

EXECUTIVE CREATIVE
DIRECTOR
JEREMY CRAIGEN

ART DIRECTOR
ROB MESSETER

COPYWRITER
MIKE CROWE

TITLE
THE GRAND TOUR
CLIENT
NATIONAL GALLERY, LONDON /
HEWLETT-PACKARD
AGENCY
THE PARTNERS

Imagine walking down the street and seeing what appears to be a Caravaggio painting in a gilt frame hanging on an exterior wall. Well, that was precisely the experience of thousands of Londoners in the summer of 2007 as no fewer than 44 full-scale, high-resolution prints – each in replica frames – of some of the National Gallery's finest works were hung in outdoor locations around central London. Each site was handpicked to complement a particular painting and also carried a plaque to convey information about the piece.

'The gallery had asked us to help raise awareness of the permanent collection, as well as highlight the technology services of sponsor, Hewlett-Packard,' explains a spokesperson at the agency responsible for the campaign, The Partners. 'Our response was to turn the brief on its head. Rather than trying to bring an audience to the gallery, we decided to take the gallery to the people.'

The project was hugely successful – with over 28,000 tour maps showing the location of the outdoor prints picked up from the gallery, and a further 24,000 downloaded from the website. Despite using no paid-for media, the campaign generated a huge amount of PR, both home and abroad, and became one of London's most talked-about summer shows. Writing in the *Observer*, journalist Rachel Cooke described the project as 'a perfect exercise, in branding terms, in simplicity. It's so much more than an ad; it's a public service, and a treat.'

ART DIRECTORS
JIM PRIOR, GREG
QUINTON

DESIGN DIRECTOR
ROBERT BALL

PROJECT MANAGERS
DONNA HEMLEY,
ANDREW WEBSTER

DESIGNERS
KEVIN LAN, PAUL
CURRAH, JAY LOCK

COPYWRITER
JIM DAVIES

WEBSITE DESIGN
DIGIT LONDON

PHOTOGRAPHY
MATT STUART, THE
PARTNERS, VARIOUS
FROM FLICKR

TITLE
LIVERPOOL WALL
CLIENT
VIRGIN TRAINS
AGENCY
MILES CALCRAFT BRIGINSHAW
DUFFY / ELVIS

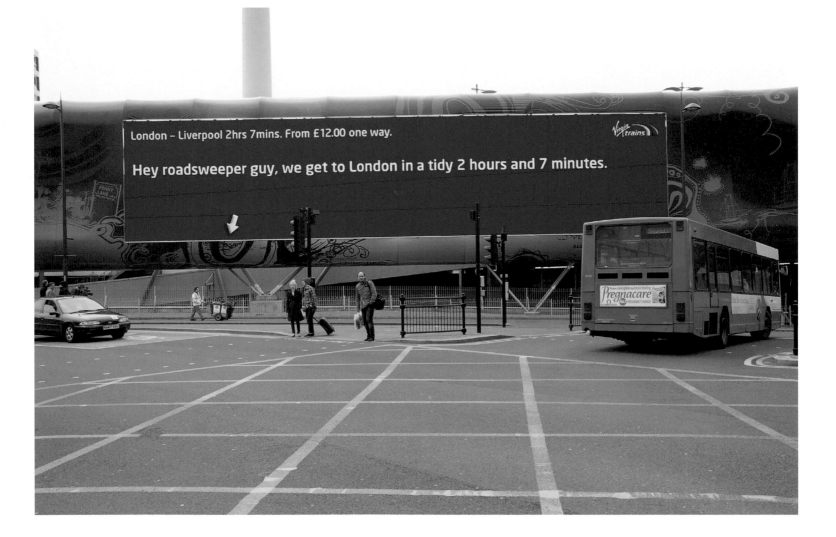

ART DIRECTOR
JOHN TREACY

COPYWRITER
RICK KIESEWETTER

DESIGNER
JASON GARFIELD

PHOTOGRAPHER
JASON GARFIELD

TYPOGRAPHER
JASON GARFIELD

PRODUCTION COMPANY
TOAST

DIRECTOR
JEREMY DUNN

BRAND PLANNER
MARY TUCKER

DIGITAL PLANNER
RICHARD NEVILLE

MEDIA AGENCY
MANNING GOTTLIEB OMD

MEDIA PLANNER
CHLOE HOWARD

CLIENT CONTACT
STEVE SEDDON
(ADVERTISING MANAGER)

In an interactive project it is usually people who do the interacting (with a device or screen), but MCBD and Elvis turned the tables by creating a digital screen – Europe's largest – that interacted with passers-by.

Creatives sitting in the building opposite the giant screen installed next to Liverpool's Lime Street Station were able to programme messages and comments to appear on the screen. Thus it appeared to be 'talking' to specific people walking or driving past, telling them about Virgin Trains' quickest ever route from Liverpool to London. There was even a cursor arrow that could point at individual people, leaving no doubt as to who each message was aimed at.

Memorable messages included one directed at a passing bus, 'By the time you get to Warrington we'll be in Euston', and another intended for a road sweeper as he wandered past, 'Hey roadsweeper guy, we get to London in a tidy 2 hours and 7 minutes'.

A representative from MCBD said: 'The unique nature of this communication meant that people couldn't miss it – especially when they were singled out in the crowd. Passers-by were amazed to see this huge media wall addressing them personally and commenting live on the scene. People cheered and even talked back to the poster.

'Given the normally non-responsive nature of outdoor, we were thrilled to discover that we saw an uplift in sales of 10% in the first week, including a massive spike of 62% on day one. Moreover, the story was picked up locally and nationally in both traditional press and online.'

THE WORLD IS NOISY ENOUGH
CLIENT
AEG ELECTROLUX
AGENCY
BBH / PERFECT FOOLS
ZENITHOPTIMEDIA
INTERNATIONAL

Large digital displays showing the current decibel level of street noise in the immediate vicinity were embedded into huge advertising spaces In London, Mllan, Brussels and Berlin. Text underneath the decibel display read, 'In a noisy world, appliances that aren't', and was accompanied by a shot of an AEG washing machine.

TITLE
SHADE
CLIENT
L'ORÉAL INDIA
AGENCY
PUBLICIS COMMUNICATIONS, MUMBAI

To promote the fact that Garnier Sun Control Daily Moisturiser contains sunblock, Publicis in Mumbai decided to advertise the product on an angled billboard designed to provide passers-by with a shady spot on a sunny day. A packshot is accompanied by the simple line, 'Protects you from the sun'. Rather like the ad itself.

CHIEF CREATIVE OFFICERS
ASHISH KHAZANCHI, PRASANNA SANKHE

CREATIVE DIRECTOR
BAPI BIT

ART DIRECTOR
DIPTI DEORUKHKAR

COPYWRITER
KARUNASAGAR SRIDHARAN

PRODUCERS
SHIREESH SABNIS, SANTOSH SHETTY

PHOTOGRAPHER
MAHESH KHATATE

ACCOUNT MANAGER
PAYAL HALWAI

ACCOUNT SUPERVISOR
DIPIKA NARAYAN

CREATIVE DIRECTORS
FELIX GLAUNER, HARALD
WITTIG, MARTIN BREUER

ART DIRECTOR
INGMAR KRANNICH

COPYWRITER
KAJO TITUS STRAUCH

DIRECTOR CLIENT
SERVICES
DIETMAR FISCHER

AGENCY PRODUCER
DETLEF STUHLDREIER

TITLE
TOILET ROLL
CLIENT
**BOEHRINGER INGELHEIM PHARMA
GMBH & CO. KG**
AGENCY
EURO RSCG DÜSSELDORF

To remind the good folk in the North Rhine–
Westphalia region of Germany that Dulcolax
is a market-leading laxative, creatives at Euro
RSCG Düsseldorf created this huge toilet
roll installation to be placed directly outside
various pharmacy stores. Apparently, during
the campaign the stores near the installations
experienced an increase in requests for
digestion-related advice.

I can't help wondering if sales of toilet roll
went up during this period too...

TITLE
CLOCKS
CLIENT
FONDS SOLIDARITÉ SIDA AFRIQUE
AGENCY
BETC EURO RSCG

In Africa, 1.6 million children and adults die from AIDS each year, nearly 4,400 people every day. Faced with this health disaster, in February 2006 the French organization Solidarité Sida (AIDS Solidarity) created a dedicated fund, the Fonds Solidarité Sida Afrique (AIDS Africa Solidarity Fund). Since then, the association has been working non-stop to provide access to more satisfactory treatment and care for the most deprived populations.

This particular installation consisted of 321 clock mechanisms arranged in such a way that at set times, twice a day, the hands of the clocks spelled out a message: 'Every 12 hours in Africa, over 2,000 people die from AIDS because they have no access to care.'

At the bottom of the installation ran the slogan, 'Every minute counts', along with the URL www.solidarite sida.org.

The installation was launched on April 30, 2009 at the Pathé Quai d'Ivry and then at the Solidays festival in June at the Longchamp Hippodrome.

Stéphane Xiberras, President and Executive Creative Director of the ad agency BETC states, 'The Clocks project has created a new way of writing an outdoor message. This is unprecedented typographic work based on an original idea from the artist Nadine Grenier. The installation casts new light on the horrendous subject of AIDS in Africa in a compelling way, from the perspective of time that goes by and kills us.'

TITLE
TRILLION DOLLAR BILLBOARD
CLIENT
THE ZIMBABWEAN
AGENCY
**TBWA \ HUNT \ LASCARIS
JOHANNESBURG**

The *Zimbabwean* newspaper started in 2005 as 'a voice for the voiceless' after Zimbabwean journalists were driven into exile for reporting how Robert Mugabe's government had rigged elections, crushed the opposition and pursued policies that caused poverty and the complete collapse of the economy. Led by London-based editor Wilf Mbanga, the paper was put together by a team of volunteers from around the world dedicated to reporting on Zimbabwean current affairs.

To raise international awareness of the paper's efforts to report on the continuing turmoil in Zimbabwe, this ingeniously satirical campaign by TBWA\Hunt\Lascaris highlights the impact of Robert Mugabe's government on Zimbabwe's economy.

The entire campaign was printed on near-worthless high-denomination Zimbabwean currency. Bundles of cash were sent to media personalities and the newspaper's contact details were printed on banknotes and attached to poster sites wherever the *Zimbabwean* was sold. Banknotes, including the ridiculous trillion dollar denomination, were also used to make outdoor murals and cover entire billboards.

It was actually cheaper to print on billions of Zimbabwean dollars than to print posters – a fact announced on one of the executions.

IT'S CHEAPER
TO PRINT THIS
ON MONEY
THAN PAPER

A VOICE FOR THE VOICELESS
TheZimbabwean

ART DIRECTORS
SHELLEY SMOLER,
NADJA LOSSGOTT

COPYWRITERS
RAPHAEL BASCKIN,
NICHOLAS HULLEY

DIRECTOR
CHLOE COETSEE

PHOTOGRAPHERS
DES ELLIS, MICHAEL
MEYERSFELD, ROB
WILSON

TRUE EVIDENCE OF WAR
UNITED NATIONS
OGILVY, STOCKHOLM

To highlight the plight of Georgia's 280,000 refugees, creatives from Ogilvy's Stockholm offices went to the country to collect various pieces of often bloody evidence of the violent and dangerous conditions there. These artefacts ranged from pieces of blood-stained clothing through to abandoned children's toys and, gruesomely, items pulled from the wreckage of a bombed pre-school.

The objects were then displayed in bus shelters around Stockholm, along with copy explaining what they were and how they had come to be abandoned. The fact that genuine artefacts were shown made the plight of Georgia's refugees all the more tangible and real for the commuters the campaign was aimed at.

The kindergarten in Gori was attacked by fighter jets. These are the remains.

"Our childhood" says the sign.
The shrapnel is from the bomb that hit the pre-school. No one knows where the surviving children are.
The civilian suffering is not over.
It has only just begun.

Help Georgia's 280 000 refugees.
Donate 5 Euros, SMS "FN" to 72900.

UN.SE

This dress was found behind an
abandoned factory in Oseti.

Every day, civilians are subjected to
assaults from the militia and robbers.
Sources say soldiers are still raping and
shooting people for fun.
The civilian suffering is not over.
It has only just begun.

Help Georgia's 280 000 refugees.
Donate 5 Euros, SMS "FN" to 72900.

UN.SE

This flight vest belonged to a pilot
who was shot down.

The blood stains come from his Kalashnikov
which speared him when he crashed.
But the war did not only affect the military.
More than 2000 civilians were killed and
thousands of people lost their homes.
The civilian suffering is not over.
It has only just begun.

Help Georgia's 280 000 refugees.
Donate 5 Euros, SMS "FN" to 72900.

UN.SE

No one knows what happened to
the Kancheli family. These are
the only remains.

In the flowerpot that stood in the kitchen
window lies a bullet left from a machine
gun. Their block was bombed to the
ground. The people who used to live there
lost everything.
The civilian suffering is not over.
It has only just begun.

Help Georgia's 280 000 refugees.
Donate 5 Euros, SMS "FN" to 72900.

UN.SE

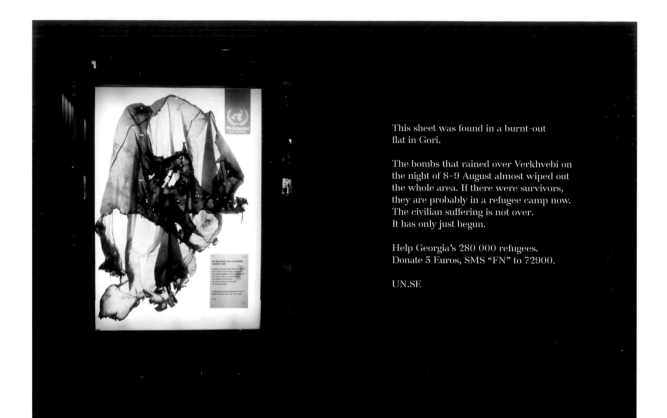

This sheet was found in a burnt-out
flat in Gori.

The bombs that rained over Verkhvebi on
the night of 8–9 August almost wiped out
the whole area. If there were survivors,
they are probably in a refugee camp now.
The civilian suffering is not over.
It has only just begun.

Help Georgia's 280 000 refugees.
Donate 5 Euros, SMS "FN" to 72900.

UN.SE

These shoes were found in a ditch
between Gori and Tbilsi.

After the war, hundreds of thousands of people
were forced to escape. Many had
to walk the roads for days.
If the woman who owned these shoes is
still alive, then she is probably in a
refugee camp now. Soon it will be winter.
The civilian suffering is not over.
It has only just begun.

Help Georgia's 280 000 refugees.
Donate 5 Euros, SMS "FN" to 72900.

UN.SE

This doll was found in a bomb-
wrecked flat in Verchlavi.

The little girl who owned it also lost
her dad. She needs help. Children without
parents have a greater risk of
being assaulted.
The civilian suffering is not over.
It has only just begun.

Help Georgia's 280 000 refugees.
Donate 5 Euros, SMS "FN" to 72900.

UN.SE

This pair of jeans were found in a
bomb-wrecked flat in Gori.

For two days, bombs rained down on the
residential district of Verkhvebi.
18 people were killed. The survivors are
now most likely in refugee camps.
The civilian suffering is not over.
It has only just begun.

Help Georgia's 280 000 refugees.
Donate 5 Euros, SMS "FN" to 72900.

UN.SE

EXECUTIVE CREATIVE
DIRECTOR
BJÖRN STÅHL

ART DIRECTOR
ATTILA KIRALY

COPYWRITERS
BJÖRN PERSSON,
MIKAEL STROM

TITLE
CUTTIN' UP

CLIENT
ALLIANCE THEATRE

AGENCY
BBDO ATLANTA

To promote the Alliance Theatre's production of *Cuttin' Up*, a play about African-American barber-shop culture which opened in early 2008, BBDO Atlanta decided to create a medium based on a classic icon that figures prominently in the play: the afro comb. Giant afro combs, each about 1.5m (5ft) tall, were created and placed in suitably shaped shrubs and bushes around Atlanta – each comb displaying the text *'Cuttin' Up*, a play about barber shops', along with the theatre's URL.

CHIEF CREATIVE OFFICER
MARCUS KEMP

CREATIVE DIRECTOR
KYLE LEWIS

COPYWRITER
PHIL GABLE

ART DIRECTOR
MARCO HOWELL

DIRECTOR OF
EXPERIENTIAL
MARKETING
DEBORAH DRAPER

AGENCY PRODUCERS
PATRICK HUDSON,
KELLY HARDEN

PRODUCTION COMPANY
ATOMIC PROPS

A few of the giant combs were actually stolen, which was just fine with us and the client. The thefts generated lots of buzz from local TV news outlets and radio personalities. The campaign boosted ticket sales by 60%.

PHIL GABLE

TITLE
LONDON INK

CLIENT
DISCOVERY REAL TIME

AGENCY
MOTHER

TATTOOISTS
LOUIS MOLLOY, DAN
GOLD, PHIL KYLE,
NIKOLE LOWE

SCULPTURE PRODUCTION
ASYLUM

To promote *London Ink*, a six-part reality series which aired on the Discovery Real Time channel and which followed celebrity tattooist Louis Molloy as he set up a tattoo parlour in London, ad agency Mother created two huge tattooed sculpted figures, which were placed in busy areas of London (near Tower Bridge and in Victoria Station) in September 2007.

Both of the figures sported suitably enormous tattoos (designed by Molloy), which played on classic tattoo iconography. The one that appeared near Tower Bridge (known as The Swimmer, for rather obvious reasons) had a tattoo featuring a Japanese Carp shown on a bed of chips and newspaper, with a splash of vinegar on top in the style of the Japanese artist Hokusai's famous print *The Great Wave*. The other statue, of a girl peering into a photo booth at Victoria Station, had a tattoo of a typical London pigeon, complete with tatty feathers and a lame foot, but styled in the form of a classic 'war eagle' motif.

The sculptural installations were supported by print, TV and cinema ads, as well as by tattoo designs stencilled on London streets. In addition, a film showing the installation of the swimmer figure at Tower Bridge appeared on YouTube.

SITE SPE-CIFIC

TITLE
BLOOD TRACES
CLIENT
INAIL
AGENCY
FABRICA

It is estimated that each year in Italy there are around 250,000 accidents in the workplace causing, on average, five deaths per day. Workers, it seems, regularly disregard safety measures.

Inail, Italy's National Workplace Safety Authority, asked Fabrica to develop a campaign aimed at raising awareness of accidental on-the-job injury. The response: bloodstain stickers placed strategically around building sites to highlight areas where accidents might happen if due care is not taken.

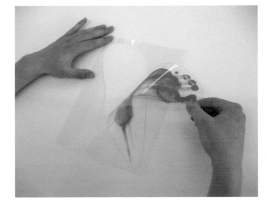

CREATIVE DIRECTOR
OMAR VULPINARI

ART DIRECTOR
LARS WANNOP

Use helmet!

INAIL

When briefed to raise awareness of testicular cancer and inform men how to detect it, McCann Erickson thought they would give men a hand – literally.

Cut-out hands in the 'cup' position were placed strategically in male strongholds, such as car washes, barber shops, male changing rooms at gyms, etc. Each hand also contained the message, 'be bold, check them!', along with a link to a supporting website (www.proverigi.com.mk), which contained further information about checking for testicular cancer. The message was even rubber-stamped on eggs in local shops. Why? Because in Macedonian slang, testicles are known as eggs!

The agency claims that awareness of testicular cancer rose from just 1% to 74% following the campaign, with an 11% increase in visits to the doctor to consult about possible cases of the disease.

TITLE
CHECK THEM

CLIENT
VERITAS SPIRITI

AGENCY
MCCANN ERICKSON, SKOPJE

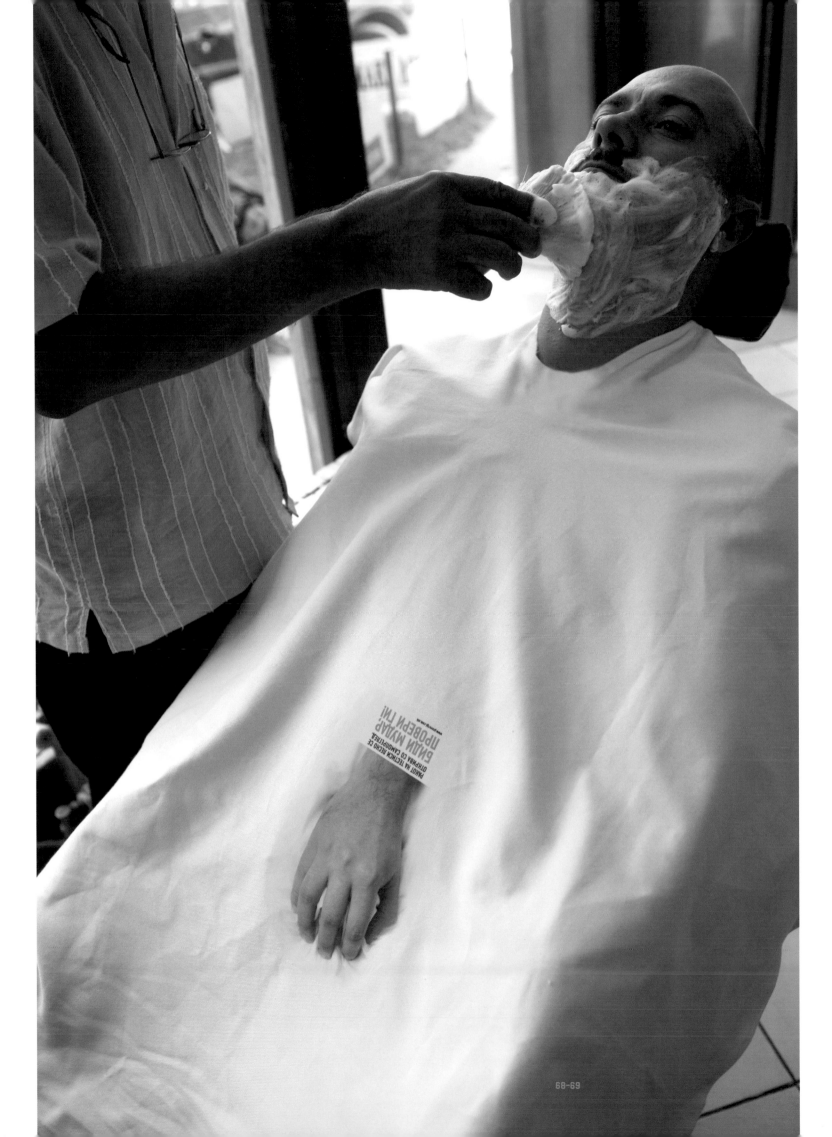

ЕДИН МУДАР ПРОВЕРИ ЛИ!

РАКОТ НА ТЕСТИКОЛ МОЖНО СЕ ОТКРИВА СО САМОПРЕГЛЕД.

www.psunij.com.au

CHAIRMAN
SRDJAN SAPER

MANAGING DIRECTOR
VLADIMIR DIMOVSKI

CREATIVE DIRECTOR
IVICA SPASOVSKI

ART DIRECTOR
VLADIMIR MANEV

PROJECT MANAGER
BILJANA PETROVA

TITLE
HENDRICK'S GIN PARAPHERNALIA
CLIENT
HENDRICK'S GIN / WILLIAM GRANT & SONS
AGENCY
HERE DESIGN

Design studio, here design, based in Hackney, east London, created a range of idiosyncratic objects that drinkers of Hendrick's Gin would encounter in various selected bars, hotels and restaurants. These objects include a bespoke porcelain tea set comprising a teapot, cup and saucer and punchbowl – which are all used to serve Hendrick's range of hot and cold cocktails; a pocket sized facsimile of Weldon's *Etiquette For Gentlemen* (originally published around 1900); wooden crates for storing cucumbers (an essential ingredient of a Hendrick's & Tonic, apparently); and a rather charming cucumber carry-case (not shown).

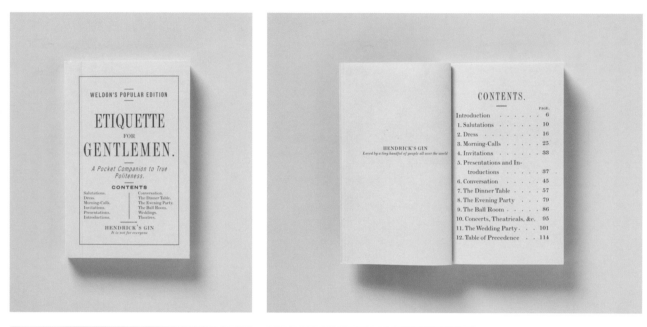

TITLE
FOOTBALL FRESCO

CLIENT
ADIDAS

AGENCY
TBWA \ BERLIN

During the German-hosted 2006 FIFA World Cup, adidas wanted to get across the message that they cooperate with the best football players on the planet. Rather than run a traditional poster campaign, the creatives at TBWA\Berlin decided it would be far more impressive to create a huge Renaissance-style fresco on the ceiling of the main lobby of Cologne Central Station.

Within minutes of the fresco's unveiling, it was featured on national German television and press covered it throughout the World Cup. More than 8.5 million people saw the fresco in the flesh during the course of the tournament.

CREATIVE DIRECTORS
STEFAN SCHMIDT, KURT-GEORG DIECKERT

ART DIRECTORS
HELGE BLÖCK, BORIS SCHWIEDRZIK

TITLE
HAVE ANY BOOKS LYING AROUND?
CLIENT
**GREENVILLE LITERARY
ASSOCIATION**
AGENCY
THE BOUNCE AGENCY

The Bounce Agency, based in Greenville, South Carolina, created this guerrilla campaign in which windows were turned into bookshelves, staircases into piles of books and post-it notes were even wrapped in miniature dust jackets – all to deliver the message that unwanted books could be donated to the Greenville Literary Association's annual Really Good, Really Big, Really Cheap Book Sale fundraising event.

CHIEF EXECUTIVE
OFFICER
CARLOS JIMENEZ

CREATIVE DIRECTOR
JOHN MCDERMOTT

ASSOCIATE CREATIVE
DIRECTOR
STEPHEN CHILDRESS

ART DIRECTORS
BARRY GODFREY,
STEPHEN BROWN

DESIGNER
MELISSA NOCKS

TRAFFIC/PRODUCTION
KRISTIN PATTERSON

PRINT PRODUCTION
AMANDA O'SULLIVAN

ACCOUNT EXECUTIVE
KATHRYN SLATE

PRINTERS
TPM, ASSOCIATED
POSTERS

The Lego Digital Box is a point-of-sale gadget which allows potential buyers of Lego toy sets to hold a box in front of a screen and see a 3D model of the box's contents appear as if sitting on the box in the user's hands. The user can then tilt and turn the box to see the product from all angles on the screen.

What's happening is that special software recognizes each Lego box, accesses the appropriate 3D animation of the relevant Lego toy and superimposes that animation onto the live video stream being filmed by the camera embedded in the Digital Box, creating an augmented reality on the screen.

Rather than looking at a box of bricks, customers get to see exactly how the contents will look when assembled. Plus it's fun to hold up the boxes and see the virtual assembled model appear as if by magic on the screen.

You can see the Digital Box in action on YouTube (http://www.youtube.com/watch?v=mUuVvY4c4-A).

TITLE
DIGITAL BOX
CLIENT
LEGO®
AGENCY
METAIO GMBH

MANAGING DIRECTOR
JAVIER CAVANILLAS

EXECUTIVE CREATIVE
DIRECTORS
JULIO GÁLVEZ, PABLO
PÉREZ-SOLERO

CREATIVE DIRECTOR
IÑIGO ANCIZU

ART DIRECTOR
RAFAEL AYUSO

COPYWRITER
SERGIO CUENCA

ACCOUNT DIRECTOR
MARTA LARRAURI

ACCOUNT EXECUTIVES
ZULEMA BLASCO,
JUAN MONTESEGURO

TITLE
LUCK IS EVERYWHERE
CLIENT
CASINO GRAN MADRID
AGENCY
BUNGALOW25

This campaign for a Madrid casino cost hardly anything to implement but ingeniously encouraged passers-by to play a simple version of the good ol' fruit machine.

The panel appeared on a pedestrian bridge over one of Madrid's busiest roads. If you could photograph three cars of the same colour – so that one appeared in each of the three windows cut into the panel – then you stood to win €80,000.

TITLE
LUNGS

CLIENT
QUIT

AGENCY
SAATCHI & SAATCHI

As smokers stubbed out their cigarettes and dropped them in these special wall-mounted outdoor ashtrays (which started appearing around London in July 2008), they had the dubious pleasure of seeing their cigarette butt join dozens more through a transparent panel that had been overlaid with an X-ray style image of a pair of lungs. The effect was that of a pair of lungs full of cigarette butts and ash. Gross.

ART DIRECTOR
DAVE ASKWITH

COPYWRITER
ROB PORTEOUS

PRODUCER
ROWENA COKAYNE

ACCOUNT HANDLER
SIMON RONCHETTI

CLIENT CONTACT
GLYN MCINTOSH,
BRAND MANAGER

A set of lungs full of cigarette butts really is a disgusting image. We hope that the campaign will encourage people to call the Quitline.

PAUL SILBURN, SAATCHI & SAATCHI

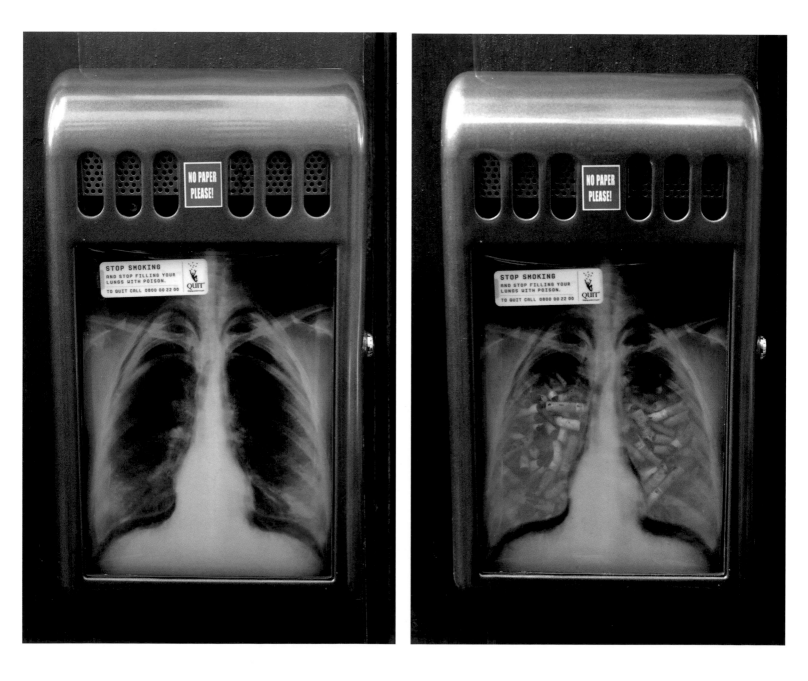

TITLE
ROASTING TIN

CLIENT
RSPCA

AGENCY
LUNAR BBDO

These chicken-shaped stickers were placed in roasting tins in selected retail outlets by agency Lunar BBDO on behalf of their client, The Royal Society for the Prevention of Cruelty to Animals (RSPCA), as part of a national campaign to encourage people to boycott cheap, factory-reared chickens in favour of free-range birds.

ART DIRECTOR
CHRISTOPHER BOWSHER

COPYWRITER
FRANCES LEACH

Some chickens get more room when they're dead than when they're alive. Cheap chickens are condemned to a life spent in overcrowded, dimly lit sheds that allow each chicken less space than an A4 sheet of paper. If it's not Freedom Food, Free Range or Organic, please don't buy it.

In the run up to Christmas 2007, Nokia sponsored the Christmas lights on Regent Street as part of a campaign to advertise the imminent arrival of its flagship London store, which was due to open at 240 Regent Street in January 2008.

Rather pleasingly, Nokia logos and textual information were abandoned in favour of these molecular-cluster type lights which were designed by United Visual Artists in collaboration with the P2 Group.

Fourteen of these light clusters lit up the famous London street. In an intriguing twist, motion cameras set up along the street monitored pedestrian traffic, and this data – along with environmental factors including wind speed, weather and ambient light levels – influenced the lights' behaviour.

TITLE
**NOKIA'S REGENT STREET
CHRISTMAS LIGHTS**

CLIENT
**REGENT STREET ASSOCIATION /
NOKIA UK**

AGENCY
WIEDEN + KENNEDY

CREATIVES
**DARREN WRIGHT,
LUCY COLLIER**

ARCHITECTURAL
INSTALLATIONS
UNITED VISUAL ARTISTS

INSTALLATION DESIGN
AND DEVELOPMENT
P2 GROUP

RIGGING
PIGGOT'S

TITLE
PARK BENCH
CLIENT
CANCER RESEARCH UK
AGENCY
OGILVYONE LONDON

The park bench pictured here was one of a series of benches placed in parks around the UK as part of a campaign by Cancer Research UK to recognize the increasing number of people surviving cancer.

Normally, park bench dedications are in memory of loved ones who have passed away. However, the inscriptions on these benches were different. They each named a genuine cancer survivor, such as the one pictured, which reads, 'Susan James loved sitting here. And still does thanks to research into cancer.' A number to call to donate to Cancer Research UK also appeared engraved on the benches.

EXECUTIVE CREATIVE DIRECTOR
COLIN NIMICK

ART DIRECTORS
**EMMA DE LA FOSSE,
CHARLIE WILSON**

TITLE
STREETMUSEUM
CLIENT
MUSEUM OF LONDON
AGENCY
BROTHERS AND SISTERS

In May 2010 the Museum of London launched an iPhone app that brings its extensive art and photographic collections to the streets of the UK capital.

The free app, called StreetMuseum, was developed with creative agency Brothers and Sisters. It makes use of geotagging and Google Maps to link historical images of London scenes from the museum's archive to the locations as shown on a map.

Here's how it works. The user opens the app and allows it to work out his or her current location. A map then opens up on screen showing not only the user's position – but also the locations of the various featured sites.

Touch one of the tags on the map and a small window opens up to describe the location and also give the date and creator of the image (below left). Click on the blue arrow on the right of this window and the image appears on screen (below centre). Tap the screen to read more about the image (below right).

The really clever thing about this app is that if you are in one of the featured locations, you can click on a '3D view' button and the app will recognize where you are and overlay the historical image over the current view through your iPhone's camera lens – augmenting the reality that the built-in iPhone camera perceives.

An engaging way to let people use the technology in their pockets to interact with the Museum of London.

Back   **Carnaby Street**

Carnaby Street

1968, Henry Grant

During the 'swinging 60s', Carnaby Street boasted many boutiques including John Stephen. Stephen opened his first shop in 1963 and went on to own nine more in Carnaby Street alone.

© Henry Grant Collection/Museum of London

EXECUTIVE CREATIVE
DIRECTOR
ANDY FOWLER

CREATIVE DIRECTOR
STEVE SHANNON

CREATIVES
KIRSTEN RUTHERFORD,
LISA JELLIFFE

DEVELOPERS
GAVIN BUTTIMORE,
ROBIN CHARLTON

HEAD OF DIGITAL
KEVIN BROWN

DIGITAL PROJECT
MANAGER
TANYA HOLLAND

DIGITAL DESIGNER
MATEUS WANDERLEY

ACCOUNT MANAGER
EMMA SIMMONS

NEW BUSINESS DIRECTOR
HELEN KIMBER

IMAGE GEOTAGGER
JACK KERRUISH

To encourage people to test drive the VW Eos convertible, creatives at DDB Düsseldorf came up with the idea of letting the sunshine do the talking. A black poster with cut-out type was carefully angled so that on sunny days it cast a shadow onto the busy pedestrian area below it, to reveal the text, 'Perfect weather for a test drive'.

TITLE
SHADOW POSTER
CLIENT
VOLKSWAGEN
AGENCY
DDB GERMANY / DÜSSELDORF

Everywhere we put it up, the
shadow poster not only caused
a stir but also increased the
number of test drives by more
than 12%. Thus the €2,000
poster generated PR to the
value of about €200,000.

DDB GERMANY / DÜSSELDORF

EXECUTIVE CREATIVE
DIRECTORS
AMIR KASSAEI,
ERIC SCHOEFFLER

CREATIVE DIRECTORS
HEIKO FREYLAND,
RAPHAEL MILCZAREK

ART DIRECTORS
FABIAN KIRNER,
MICHAEL KITTEL

COPYWRITERS
FELIX LEMCKE,
JAN PROPACH

AGENCY PRODUCER
MICHAEL FRIXE

ACCOUNT MANAGER/
STRATEGIC PLANNER
SILKE LAGODNY

As part of a campaign to encourage the people of San Francisco's Bay Area to be prepared in case of earthquakes, huge mobile billboards were deployed, each one depicting landmark buildings and streets in a state of collapse as if photographed after a powerful and devastating earthquake. The billboards were positioned so that passers-by might be fooled into thinking they were looking at a real scene.

A message at the bottom of each billboard read: 'What do we have to do to get your attention? Be prepared. Visit redcrossbayarea.org.'

TITLE
WHAT DO WE HAVE TO DO TO GET YOUR ATTENTION?

CLIENT
AMERICAN RED CROSS

AGENCY
PUBLICIS & HAL RINEY

CREATIVE DIRECTOR
JON SOTO

ART DIRECTOR
DOMINIC GOLDMAN

COPYWRITER
MARK SWEENEY

PHOTOGRAPHER
MATTHEW WELCH

ART PRODUCER
PATRICIA HOM

RETOUCHING
IMAGIC

PROJECT MANAGER
KRISTINA LEES

TITLE
WHAT DO WE HAVE TO DO TO GET YOUR ATTENTION?

CLIENT
AMERICAN RED CROSS

AGENCY
PUBLICIS & HAL RINEY

CREATIVE DIRECTOR
JON SOTO

ART DIRECTOR
DOMINIC GOLDMAN

COPYWRITER
MARK SWEENEY

PHOTOGRAPHER
MATTHEW WELCH

ART PRODUCER
PATRICIA HOM

RETOUCHING
IMAGIC

PROJECT MANAGER
KRISTINA LEES

TITLE
ALIEN FIRE EXTINGUISHERS
CLIENT
TABLE MOUNTAIN NATIONAL PARK
AGENCY
ANIMAL FARM

CREATIVES
PORKY HEFER,
WARREN LEWIS

PRODUCER
LISA MAHONY

SPONSORS
CAPE UNION MART AND
ANIMAL FARM

Each summer, large swathes of Cape Town's forests are destroyed by fire and, unfortunately, the local fire department just doesn't have the resources to deal with the situation.

The truth is, once a fire has started in a tinder-dry forest, it's almost impossible to put it out, which is why Table Mountain National Park commissioned this fire-prevention awareness campaign. Cape Town agency Animal Farm decided to attach carved wooden fire extinguishers, complete with fire-prevention information and advice, to trees throughout the park – 'the main idea being that a wooden fire extinguisher would be as effective as a real one if you were trying to stop a wildfire,' explained Porky Hefer of Animal Farm. 'Our hope was to create a general awareness around fire prevention,' he says.

The agency commissioned The Carpenter's Shop, an NGO set up to teach woodwork skills to the homeless and unemployed, to create 65 extinguishers in total. It was decided that they should be carved from alien species of pine introduced to the environment by settlers and traders from the northern hemisphere within the last two or three centuries. This choice of wood itself carried an important message, as the alien pines are held to be one of the factors responsible for creating the dry conditions in which forest fires are more likely: 'These are the trees that drink all the water, suck up all the light and most of all spread their seed when they burn,' points out Hefer.

TITLE
WRONG WORKING ENVIRONMENT
CLIENT
JOBSINTOWN.DE
AGENCY
SCHOLZ & FRIENDS, BERLIN

CREATIVE DIRECTORS
MATTHIAS SPAETGENS,
OLIVER HANDLOS

ART DIRECTORS
DAVID FISCHER,
TABEA RAUSCHER

COPYWRITERS
DANIEL BOEDEKER,
AXEL TISCHER

PHOTOGRAPHER
HANS STARCK

AGENCY PRODUCER
SOEREN GESSAT

GRAPHICS
FERDINAND ULRICH,
JULIA HAUCH

ACCOUNT MANAGERS
KATRIN VOSS,
SASCHA KRUSE

Skilfully art-directed posters designed to fit on the sides of specific service machines revealed the fictitious interior of each machine, in which a person was working in cramped conditions, supposedly slogging his or her guts out to make the device function.

The message was simple: 'Life's too short for the wrong job'. The posters also displayed the URL of jobsintown.de – a web destination where visitors can browse hundreds of available jobs across dozens of industries.

Life's too
short for the
wrong job.

jobsintown.de

Life's too short
for the wrong job.

jobsintown de

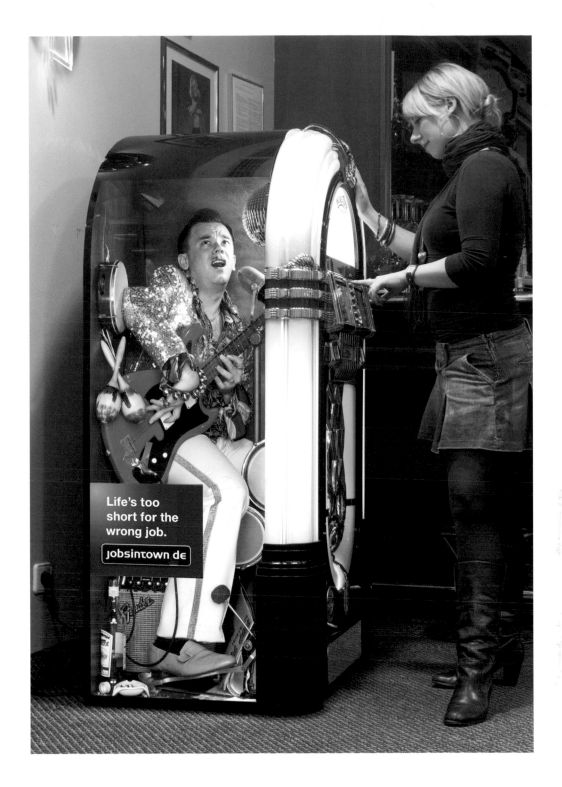

TITLE
TAKE THE NIGHT BUS

CLIENT
DE LIJN

AGENCY
DUVAL GUILLAUME

A truly guerrilla campaign, the idea here was
to hijack flyposters for clubnights and other
late-night events by surrounding them with a
rectangular frame sticker, which advertised the
late-night bus service as a means of getting
home afterwards. In this way the original
poster became the visual element of what was
essentially a new poster.

The copy along the bottom of the frame
read: 'Whatever you're planning tonight, plan
your transport too. Take the night bus.'

CREATIVE DIRECTORS
PETER AMPE,
KATRIEN BOTTEZ

ART DIRECTOR
SVEN VAN HOOYDONCK

COPYWRITER
GEERARD VAN DE WALLE

ACCOUNT MANAGERS
MATTHIAS DUBOIS,
TOM SNEPPE

SNEAKY MANOEUVRES

TITLE
AC/DC ROCKS THE OFFICE

CLIENT
COLUMBIA RECORDS

AGENCY
SONY MUSIC CREATIVE

This book is primarily about unusual message-delivery systems employed by brands and their advertising agencies to reach a particular audience in a way that is appropriate, original, engaging – and often surprising. And so it is that this music promo for AC/DC's seventeenth studio album, *Black Ice*, comes to be included here. It was delivered via the most unlikely of media: an Excel spreadsheet.

'We knew from Columbia's consumer insight that our target audience of 30–40 year old men uses music like AC/DC's to escape from the stresses and boredom of everyday life,' explains Phil Clandillon, one half of the creative team that conjured up the campaign. 'Our brief was to reach this audience through the web and to provide them with a genuine "blow-out moment" in these serious times. Furthermore, we needed to let them know more practical stuff, like what the new album was called and where they could listen to it and purchase it.'

Wanting to reach the target audience at a time in their day when they would be most likely to feel the need to escape, Clandillon and creative partner Steve Milbourne decided that the obvious place would be the office – where most people are online all day anyway. Realizing that most employees are subjected to fairly restrictive internet usage and security policies, the pair decided that YouTube simply wouldn't work, as the site might well be blocked by corporate firewalls.

'We realized that by including AC/DC's music in an Excel spreadsheet, it would be able to pass through corporate firewalls unimpeded,' says Milbourne of their big idea. 'The next challenge was to make the content of the spreadsheet so compelling that people would want to talk about it, and share it with their friends. We decided to render the video for "Rock 'n' Roll Train" as ASCII art and display it directly in the cells of the spreadsheet, thus creating the world's first music video in Excel format.'

The agency created the following elements: a spreadsheet containing the music video, preview links for all of the tracks from the album and links to purchase the album online; a mini-site at www.acdcrocks.com/excel so that people could download the spreadsheet; and a video showing the music video playing in Excel, which was uploaded to AC/DC's YouTube channel. This video was used to plug the link for the campaign's website and to invite viewers to download the spreadsheet to try it for real. This helped dispel any notions that the footage might be fake as well as giving press and bloggers something they could embed in their stories when covering the campaign.

So how was the campaign received? The video that showed the spreadsheet in action has had over 1.7 million YouTube views, 500,000 of which came in the first two weeks after the campaign launch. The spreadsheet itself has been downloaded over a million times and the interaction rate on the preview links in the spreadsheet was an incredible 31%. The industry average for banner advertising is 0.05%.

'We conservatively estimate we have reached at least 3 million people through online and offline media coverage [of this campaign], helping to propel *Black Ice* to number one in the UK and number one in the pan-European top 100,' says Clandillon.

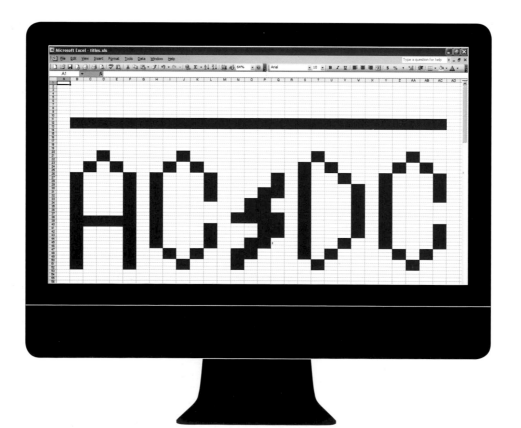

CREATIVE DIRECTORS
PHIL CLANDILLON,
STEVE MILBOURNE

PROGRAMMER
SVETOZAR BATOEU

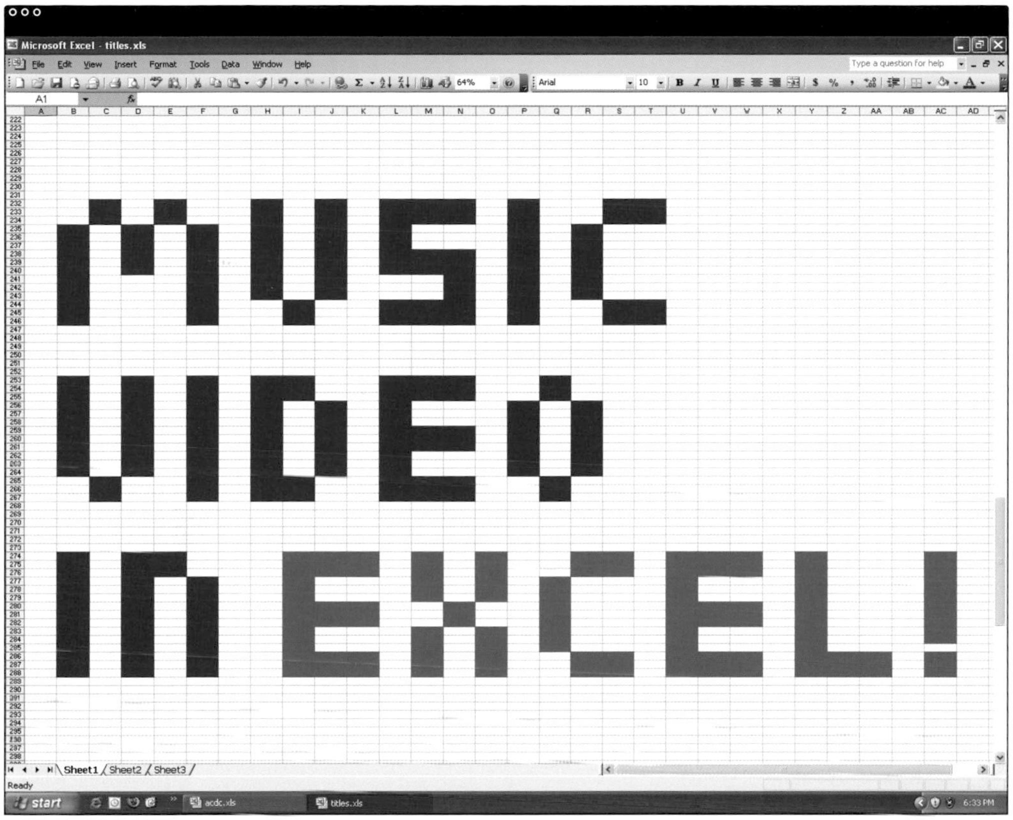

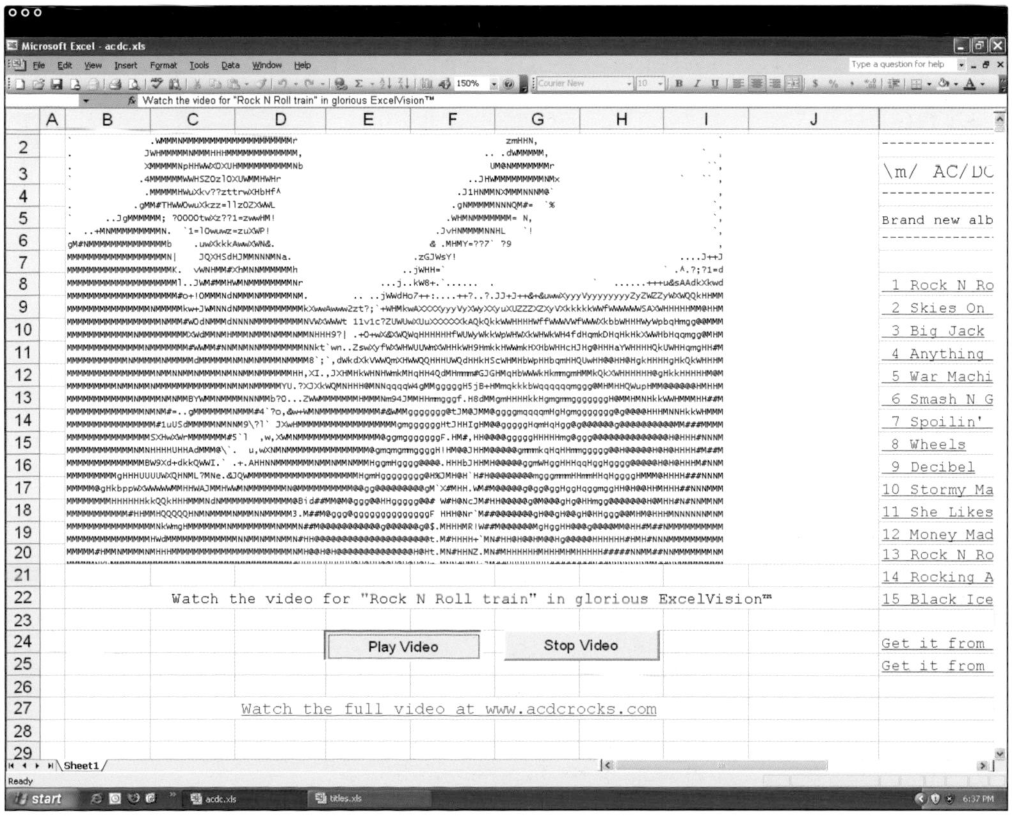

TITLE
**DATE RAPE AWARENESS
UMBRELLA**
CLIENT
WATCHYOURDRINK.COM
AGENCY
TBWA \ LONDON

While bar drinkers weren't looking, cocktail umbrellas bearing the message, 'this is how easy it is to spike your drink', were slipped into drinks glasses, thus warning the umbrellas' recipients of the dangers of drug rape. Alarming but effective message delivery!

PHOTOGRAPHER
EUGENIO FRANCHI

The whole idea of doing something that gets your brand to behave, be seen and be where their audience is, unsurprisingly seems to work. [This campaign] is definitely more impactful than a TV awareness ad that's hardly going to engage you whilst you're safe on your couch.

LIZ DEWHURST, PR MEDIA BLOG

TITLE
HEATHROW: THE BOOK

CLIENT
BAA

AGENCY
MISCHIEF

Mischief were briefed to support Heathrow's 'making every journey better' brand proposition and build consumer empathy with the owners of the airport, BAA, a corporation that was routinely accused of being secretive and unfriendly. The agency persuaded BAA to appoint a writer-in-residence to tell the story of a week at Heathrow, the idea being that the resulting book would help to humanize the airport by capturing the emotions of the people who work there and the passengers who pass through it.

Swiss-born, London-based writer Alain de Botton (pictured opposite) was hired for the task. He spent a week in the airport, having numerous meetings with passengers and airport staff – from BAA chief executive Colin Matthews to baggage operators – and much of his time was spent at a writing desk in Heathrow Terminal 5, thus providing thousands of passengers with an opportunity to talk to him and possibly become a character in the book.

Extracts of the book were read over the airport's public address system and 10,000 free copies were given out to passengers before it went on general sale.

Now, you might be forgiven, at this stage, for wondering, 'who's got time to read this book and thus engage with the exercise?'

Well, really, to ask that question is to miss the point. According to Mischief, such an unusual approach to a marketing brief garnered no fewer than 316 separate pieces of news footage. Over 250 national and international newspapers covered the story, including the *Guardian*, *The Times*, the *Daily Telegraph*, *Le Temps* and *El Pais*, and there was even an eight-page feature in *The Sunday Times*. Over 50 radio and TV interviews were conducted with de Botton at the airport (it's a wonder he got any work done at all), with broadcasters including BBC Breakfast News, BBC Radio 4's *Today* programme, CNN, BBC World Service, Sky News and the BBC *Culture Show*.

A Week At The Airport: A Heathrow Diary reached number 48 in the Amazon book chart only two days after launch. It is now being sold in over 50 countries worldwide. Mainly in rival airports.

CREATIVE DIRECTOR
DANIEL GLOVER

COVER DESIGN
DAVID PEARSON

LAYOUT DESIGN
**JOANA NIEMEYER,
APRIL STUDIO**

CLIENT CONTACT
CAT JORDAN

TITLE

TITLE
KETCHUP

CLIENT
CAMPAIGN AGAINST LANDMINES

AGENCY
**PUBLICIS MOJO,
AUCKLAND**

Over 50,000 of these ketchup sachets were produced by Publicis Mojo in 2006 for client Campaign Against Landmines (CALM, calm.org.nz) as a graphic way to convey the hideousness of the injuries that can result from stepping on a landmine – a regular occurrence in 89 countries around the world. The sachets were distributed in fast-food outlets, restaurants, bars and pubs and served with politicians' meals in embassies and political summit meetings. They also appeared as tip-ins in magazine ads.

The idea for the campaign is simple and rather clever: one side of the sachet features a photograph of a child's legs with the marked tear-off section cutting across one of the ankles just above the child's boot. Thus, when the sachet is opened, the foot is severed and blood-red ketchup gushes forth.

As well as featuring in numerous newspapers and magazines throughout New Zealand and internationally, [the campaign] increased donations to CALM from the previous year's campaign by over 300%.

PUBLICIS MOJO

CREATIVES
EMMANUEL BOUGNERES,
GUY DENNISTON,
MATTHIEU ELKAIM

PRODUCER
SACHA LOVERICH

PHOTOGRAPHER
PAUL JONES

ACCOUNT DIRECTOR
FLEUR HEAD

Brands funding the creation of entertainment content and feature films isn't a new idea – but when it's done right, it's worth celebrating.

Somers Town was the first release from a new division of Mother advertising agency, called Mother Vision, the aim of which is to create 'entertainment ideas and non-traditional communications', and it was funded by Eurostar as part of the launch of the new high-speed rail link between London and mainland Europe.

The refreshing thing about *Somers Town* is that there's no glaring Eurostar branding. The film's promotional poster mentions the company, but only in small print. There isn't even a logo to be seen in the opening credits of the movie. But the train service does form an important part of the story.

Directed by Shane Meadows, whose previous works include the acclaimed *This Is England*, the film tells the story of Tommo, a young runaway from Nottingham who arrives at King's Cross and makes friends with Marek, a Polish teenager whose father is working on the building of the Eurostar terminal at neighbouring St Pancras Station. They goof around together and try to win the affections of a young French waitress working in a King's Cross café. Towards the end of the film the boys travel to Paris (by Eurostar) in search of the waitress, who has returned to France.

It's easy to be cynical about brands funding films. However, Mother's decision to work with Meadows was a good one. This is brand-funded content at its most credible.

TITLE
SOMERS TOWN
CLIENT
EUROSTAR
AGENCY
MOTHER VISION

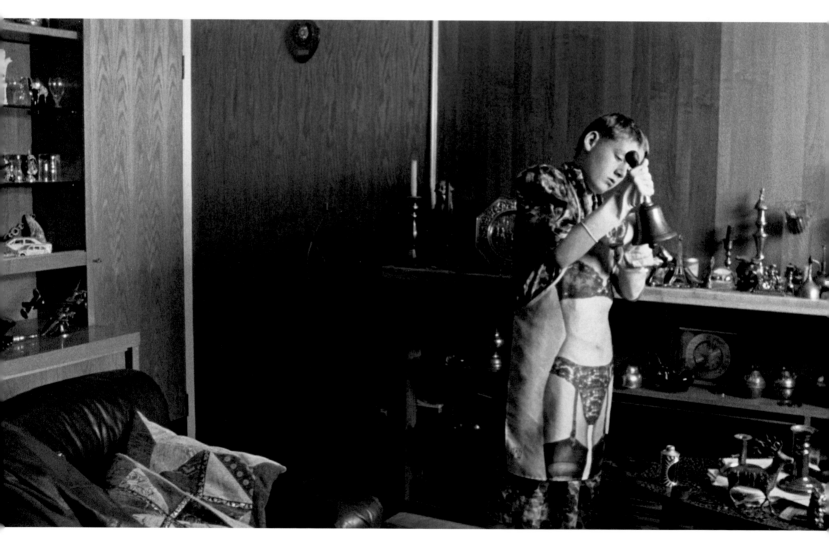

ART DIRECTION
MOTHER VISION

SCREENWRITER
PAUL FRASER

DISTRIBUTION
OPTIMUM RELEASING

PRODUCTION COMPANY
TOMBOY FILMS

DIRECTOR
SHANE MEADOWS

PRODUCER
BARNABY SPURRIER

EDITOR
RICHARD GRAHAM

POST-PRODUCTION
THE MILL

MUSIC
GAVIN CLARK

CLIENT CONTACTS
GREG NUGENT,
NICK MERCER

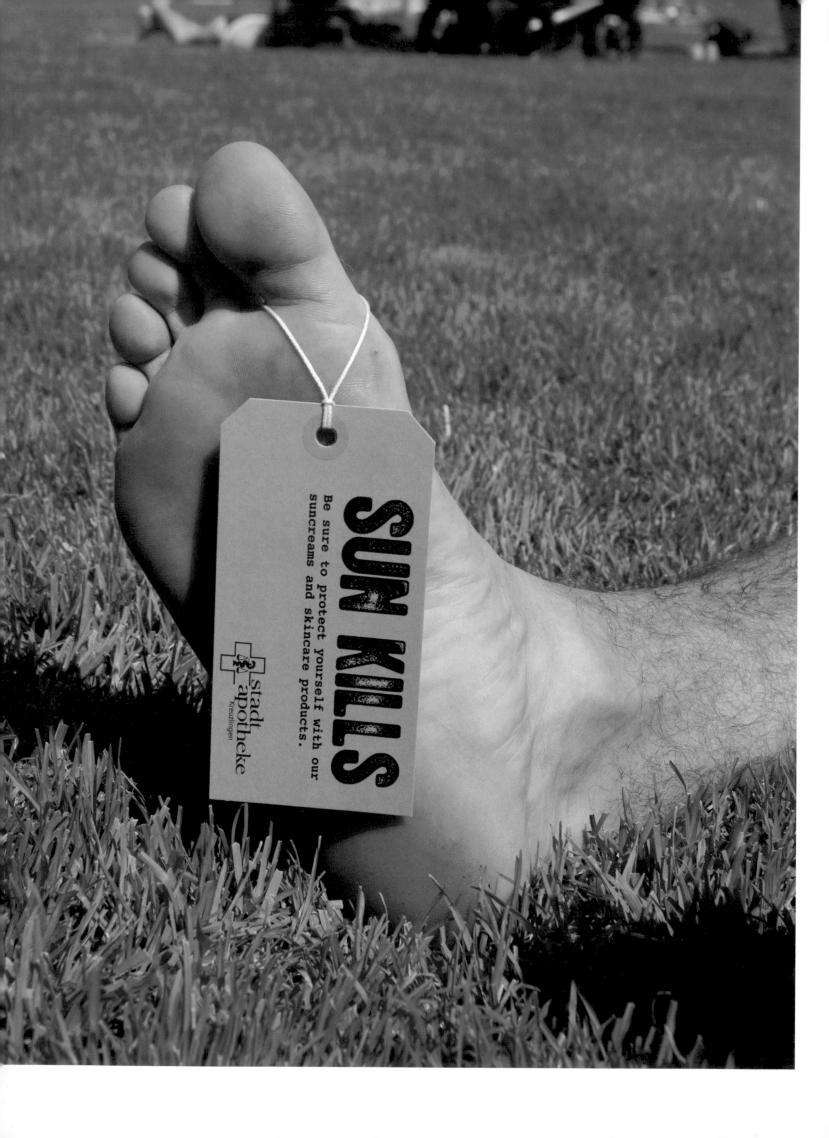

SUN KILLS

Be sure to protect yourself with our suncreams and skincare products.

stadt apotheke
Kreuzlingen

TITLE
SUN KILLS

CLIENT
STADT APOTHEKE, KREUZLINGEN

AGENCY
WIRZ / BBDO, SWITZERLAND

On a hot day in July 2008, tags were placed on the toes of anyone seen to be sleeping in the sun in Zurich's largest public park – thus giving it a somewhat macabre makeover. Sunbathers suddenly resembled corpses.

The sleeping sunbathers woke up to find the message 'sun kills' on the tags attached to their toes, along with a logo for pharmaceutical store Stadt Apotheke and a further message that read 'be sure to protect yourself with our suncreams and skincare products'.

CREATIVE DIRECTOR
MATTHIAS FREULER

ART DIRECTOR
KIM SOKOLA

COPYWRITER
TOM ZÜRCHER

CO-EXECUTIVE CREATIVE DIRECTORS
ROB REILLY, ANDREW KELLER

INTERACTIVE EXECUTIVE CREATIVE DIRECTOR
JEFF BENJAMIN

CREATIVE DIRECTORS
BILL WRIGHT, JAMES DAWSON-HOLLIS

INTERACTIVE ASSOCIATE CREATIVE DIRECTORS
NUNO FERREIRA, NEIL HEYMANN

INTERACTIVE DESIGN DIRECTOR
PELUN CHEN

INTERACTIVE DESIGNER
JOHN WHITMORE

INTERACTIVE ART DIRECTOR
SAMAN RAHMANIAN

INTERACTIVE COPYWRITER
JOEL KAPLAN

EXECUTIVE INTEGRATED PRODUCER
ROBERT VALDES

FLASH DESIGNER
ANDREW KENNEDY

PROGRAMMERS
JIMMY PINO, ROBERT CHRIST

TECHNICAL DIRECTOR
SCOTT PRINDLE

INTERACTION DIRECTOR
MATT WALSH

INTEGRATED HEAD OF INTERACTIVE VIDEO
WINSTON BINCH

INTEGRATED PRODUCER
ROB ALLEN

ASSOCIATE TECHNICAL DIRECTOR
MAT RANAURO

INTERACTION DESIGNER
JORDAN CLAYTON-HALL

TECHNICAL LEAD
OSCAR LLARENA

QUALITY ASSURANCE
JAMES LUKENSOW, STEWART WARNER

TITLE
WHOPPER SACRIFICE

CLIENT
BURGER KING

AGENCY
CRISPIN PORTER BOGUSKY

At the time of writing, it seems that almost everyone has a social networking account – and uses it to share information with their friends and family. Brands struggle to use social networking sites in a way that's clever or inventive but, despite the fact that it ran for just one week, Whopper Sacrifice remains one of the best brand campaigns ever conducted via a social networking site.

Whopper Sacrifice was an app, which users could install on their personal profile page. The app encouraged users to remove or 'sacrifice' friends from their account and, in fact, rewarded participants with a coupon for a free Whopper burger for every ten 'sacrificed' friends. Meanwhile, each of the ten friends who had been ditched received a message notifying them that the user had discarded their friendship in favour of a tenth of a free Whopper.

Within four days of the launch of Whopper Sacrifice on January 5, 2009, tens of thousands of friends had been sacrificed

and the campaign was spreading virally at an astonishing rate. In just a week, around 82,000 people had used the app to delete over 233,000 friendships. And this is when the site itself decided to step in and request that the app functioned slightly differently, and didn't notify people when their friendships were being sacrificed. Which of course was the fun part of the campaign. Basically, the notion of deleting friendships went against the company's business plan of encouraging people to make (rather than cancel) connections with others. Rather than have it continue with restrictions on its functionality, Burger King and the app's developers decided to conclude the campaign. After only one week.

Whopper Sacrifice is still talked about as being one of the best, most inventive uses of social networking by a brand.

CREATIVE DIRECTOR
TIM HURLES

DESIGNER
EOIN TIERNEY

COPYWRITER
STEVE DEMPSEY

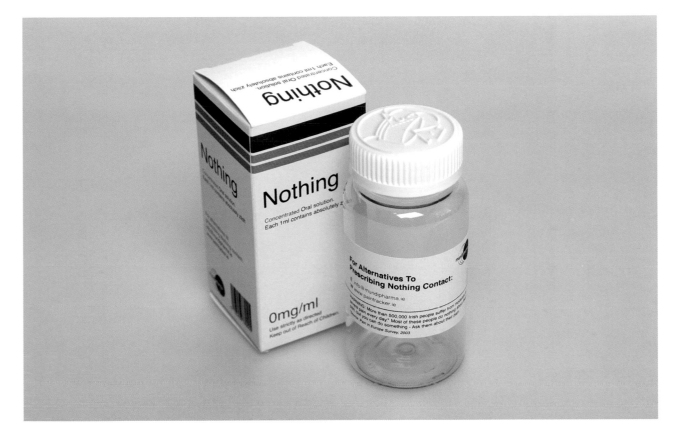

TITLE
NOTHING

CLIENT
MUNDIPHARMA

AGENCY
IO

Pharmaceutical company Mundipharma commissioned Dublin-based agency io to help them communicate to doctors the results of a survey they had conducted which had found that around half a million Irish people suffer from moderate to severe pain every day – most of whom take no medication whatsoever, suffering in silence, afraid to raise the issue with their doctors.

The agency's response was to create something that would possibly sit on doctors' desks for far longer than a letter or a more typical piece of direct mail. The idea was to make a prescription package for Nothing. Nothing came in a plastic bottle with a generic label and clean, simple packaging. The copy outlined just what the medication contained – nada – and explained that this was what many Irish people took for chronic pain on a daily basis. The finished product was sent out to doctors' surgeries nationwide and also left behind by Mundipharma reps when visiting doctors and hospitals.

TITLE
LANDMINE STICKERS
CLIENT
**UNICEF DEUTSCHLAND,
ARBEITSGRUPPE FRANKFURT**
AGENCY
LEO BURNETT, FRANKFURT

Circular stickers, with the sticky side
camouflaged so they wouldn't be noticed,
were placed, sticky side up, on busy public
concourses. As a pedestrian stepped on one
of the stickers, so it became stuck to his or
her shoe. When removing the sticker, the
pedestrian would see the non-sticky side,
designed to look like a landmine, which carried
the following message: 'In many other countries
you would now be mutilated! Help the victims
of landmines.'

EXECUTIVE CREATIVE
DIRECTOR
ANDREAS PAULI

ASSOCIATE EXECUTIVE
CREATIVE DIRECTOR
KERRIN NAUSCH

CREATIVE DIRECTORS
**ANDREAS HEINZEL,
PETER STEGER**

ART DIRECTOR
CLAUDIA BÖCKLER

COPYWRITERS
**FLORIAN KROEBER,
JEANETTE BOHNÉ**

PHOTOGRAPHY
HEINE/LENZ/ZIZKA

PRODUCER
THORSTEN ZEH

ART BUYER
CORNELIA RICHTER

DESIGNERS
**EVA MÜNSTERMANN,
TOBIAS NIENTIEDT**

ACCOUNT MANAGER
ANDREA ULLRICH

CLIENT CONTACTS
**HUBERT LEITSCH,
DIRK MOMMERTZ**

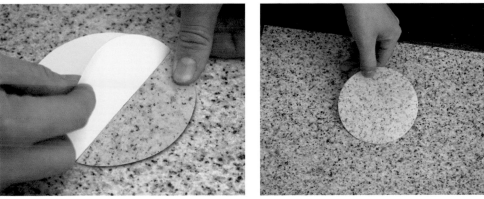

STUNTS

TITLE
ANTI-CAR

CLIENT
FLYGBUSSARNA AIRPORT COACHES

AGENCY
ACNE ADVERTISING, STOCKHOLM

This enormous 24-m (79-ft) long coach installation made out of 50 cars was located next to the major highway connecting Stockholm and its main airport, Arlanda.

The idea was to persuade travellers to and from the airport to use the airport coach service rather than make the journey by car – and what better persuasive tactic than to highlight the environmental benefit of making such a choice? Research revealed that on average each car on the road carries 1.2 people and this provided the insight that informed the campaign. An airport bus can take over 50 people, so what's better: 50 cars making a journey, or one coach?

The huge sculpture formed the centrepiece in an integrated campaign which also incorporated a website that combined a live stream of the installation and the highway in front of it with a display that calculated the potential reduction in CO_2 emissions if the people travelling past by car had chosen to use the airport coach instead.

During the first couple of days, the campaign generated a two-minute segment on a national television news show and hourly radio reports over the course of three days warning about the traffic jams caused by the installation. It also reached major newspapers, advertising and environmental media, blogs and various international titles.

CREATIVE DIRECTOR
ADAM SPRINGFELDT

ART DIRECTOR
JOHAN HOLMGEN

COPYWRITER
ERIK BERGQVIST

SET DESIGNERS
**URBAN LISINSKI
(DEKORKLIPPAN), JOHAN
SJÖLIN (ART 'N DITO)**

PHOTOGRAPHY
JOHAN WARDEN / SKARP

ACCOUNT MANAGER
SOFIA ORRHEIMN

TITLE
TREE OF SOULS
CLIENT
**TWENTIETH CENTURY FOX
HOME ENTERTAINMENT**
AGENCY
BEATWAX

In James Cameron's hugely successful *Avatar* film, which is set on the fictional planet of Pandora, the Tree of Souls is the willow-like physical connection for Pandora's Na'vi people with the planet's life force and deity, Eywa. Eywa functions a bit like a huge biological internet – with the tree acting like a computer server that stores memories. The Na'vi (and the other creatures that inhabit the planet) can plug themselves physically into the tree to upload or download memories, keeping them connected with their ancestors as well as with all living things on the planet.

To promote the release of *Avatar* on DVD in 2010, London agency Beatwax installed a giant interactive model of the Tree of Souls in London's Hyde Park.

The Tree of Souls installation was erected in the park's famous Speakers' Corner for just one weekend, from 24–26 April. During that time visitors were able to plug their phones or iPods into one of the many fibre-optic branches and upload messages to an inbuilt screen, listen to other users' music, change the colour of the optic fibres or make them move to their own music. The installation was built using a whopping 20 miles of fibre-optic cable.

In keeping with one of the central themes of the *Avatar* movie, every time someone interacted with the Tree of Souls installation through their phone or iPod, Twentieth Century Fox pledged to plant a real tree as part of a global campaign to plant a million trees worldwide.

The Tree of Souls in Hyde Park was unveiled by actor Stephen Lang, who plays Colonel Miles Quaritch in the film. Lang was in London at the time to take part in an interview and DVD signing session at HMV on nearby Oxford Street as part of the DVD launch.

TITLE
CRATEFAN
CLIENT
COCA-COLA
AGENCY
ANIMAL FARM

Designed by Cape Town creative consultancy
Animal Farm, Cratefan was a 16.5-m (54-ft)
tall, 25-tonne 'fan man' made using 2,500
standard Coca-Cola bottle crates. Cratefan
appeared in Mary Fitzgerald Square in
Newtown, Johannesburg Central and also at
the V&A Waterfront in Cape Town during the
2010 World Cup in South Africa.

CREATIVE DIRECTOR
PORKY HEFER

PROJECT MANAGEMENT
LESLEY PERKES, MARK
SINOFF, ART AT WORK
ART MANAGEMENT

REGIONAL CREATIVE
PRESIDENT
NILS ANDERSSON

GROUP EXECUTIVE
CREATIVE DIRECTOR
FOREST YOUNG

EXECUTIVE CREATIVE
DIRECTORS
YUAN ZHONG, MATTHEW
CURRY, SONG YUE,
KWEICHEE LAM,
ECHO LEE

CREATIVE DIRECTORS
FOREST YOUNG, LENA
HOU, ROCKY REN,
YU ZHENHUA, BILLY LU

COPYWRITERS
LAO BAI, JOHNNY PAN,
WOLF LIU

PHOTOGRAPHER
CHAO WEI

EDITORIAL COMPANY
MERCERA GUO,
STONE YANG

民工孩子读书难

新公民计划

TITLE
ILLITERIT
CLIENT
NEW CITIZEN PROGRAM
AGENCY
OGILVY, BEIJING

Visitors to the Song Zhuang Art Gallery, Beijing, were faced with a strange-looking artwork consisting of a circular area on the concourse outside the gallery covered in hundreds of shards of glass. At the centre of the circle, and very much out of reach, sat an open book. A small plaque explained: 'For millions of kids, education is out of reach'. Under the headline was a number to call if people wished to donate to the New Citizen Program – an organization dedicated to highlighting the plight of the millions of children who relocate with their migrant worker parents to China's big cities.

This was one of several art installations on this theme commissioned from local artists by Ogilvy on behalf of the New Citizen Program. Another, called Barbed Wire, consisted of a giant ball of barbed wire, again with an open book visible at its centre. The same message accompanied it.

At the time of writing, enough money had been raised through donations made by people responding to the sculptures to commission the building of a new school and enrol 950 students.

CREATIVE DIRECTOR
STEFAN SCHMIDT

ART DIRECTORS
**MARCO BEZERRA,
EMILIANO TREIERVEILER**

TITLE
IMPOSSIBLE GOALKEEPER
CLIENT
ADIDAS
AGENCY
TBWA \ BERLIN

Just before the start of the UEFA EURO 2008 football tournament, adidas turned one of Vienna's best-known landmarks, the Prater ferris wheel, into a huge image of the Czech national goalkeeper, Petr Čech. At a whopping 53m (174ft) tall, this gigantic installation was visible far beyond the Prater entertainment park and the nearby public viewing sites. In the installation, Čech had eight arms that constantly rotated with the ferris wheel.

The erection of the metal construction started on May 13 and was finished just before the launch of the tournament on the night of June 5, 2008. This advertising landmark also hosted the official adidas press conference prior to the tournament.

TITLE
MAN TRAPPED IN PINT GLASS
CLIENT
**THINK! ROAD SAFETY /
DEPARTMENT FOR TRANSPORT**
AGENCY
LEO BURNETT

Agency Leo Burnett did some research and found that anti-drink-driving advertising based around crashing and injury was no longer likely to affect the target demographic of young male drivers who don't believe that driving after drinking a couple of beers is dangerous. The agency found that low-consumption male drink-drivers were more likely to be deterred by the personal consequences of a drink-driving conviction.

The idea of this campaign was to play against the seasonal jollity of the Christmas period and to dramatize the experience of isolation, regret and stigmatization brought about by a drink-driving conviction. In December 2007 a real-life convicted drink-driver agreed to be placed inside a specially constructed upturned pint glass. He was thus trapped by his seemingly innocuous decision to get behind the wheel after having one pint too many. The subject was interviewed by national press and broadcast media in Paddington Station as he explained how being convicted of

a drink-driving offence had ruined his life – he had lost his job, his girlfriend, his car and a lot of money. An actor then took over the role of the drink-driver up and down the country at locations specially chosen for their proximity to public car parks and areas with a high concentration of pubs and bars (particularly those used by football fans).

The campaign is thought to have contributed to a drop of 20% in breath test failures during the pre-Christmas period of 2007.

CREATIVE DIRECTORS
**TONY MALCOLM,
GUY MOORE**

CREATIVES
**PHILLIP DEACON,
BERTIE SCRASE**

PLANNING DIRECTOR
NICK DOCHERTY

EXPERIENTIAL AGENCY
LIME

PR AGENCY
RED

TITLE
WOMAN IN A SUITCASE
CLIENT
AMNESTY INTERNATIONAL
AGENCY
SERVICEPLAN

Incredibly, this guerrilla stunt saw a real woman placed inside a transparent suitcase which was put onto busy luggage-claim carousels in German airports. The luggage had two yellow stickers – one that clearly identified it as an Amnesty International campaign and another that read 'Stoppt Menschenhandel!' – a protest against human trafficking.

The campaign was picked up by 58 different daily newspapers, magazines and news portals.

EXECUTIVE CREATIVE
DIRECTOR
MATTHIAS HARBECK

CREATIVE DIRECTORS
HELMUT HUBER, FLORIAN
DRAHORAD

ART DIRECTORS
CHRISTIAN SOMMER,
IVO HLAVAC

COPYWRITER
NICOLAS BECKER

CONSULTANTS
MICHAEL FREITAG,
BRITTA CHRISTOPH

ADVERTISER'S
SUPERVISOR
ANNE-CATHERINE
PAULISCH

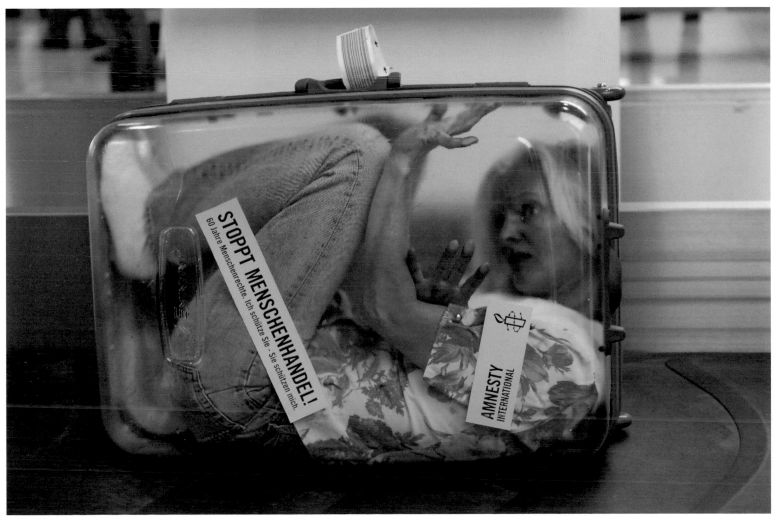

TITLE
IMPOSSIBLE HUDDLE
CLIENT
ADIDAS
AGENCY
TBWA \ BERLIN

CREATIVE DIRECTORS
STEFAN SCHMIDT,
MARKUS EWERTZ

ART DIRECTORS
ERIK GONAN, HENDRIK
SCHWEDER

For the duration of the UEFA EURO 2008 football tournament, TBWA\Berlin transformed the main hall of Zurich's Central Station into a large-scale celebration of team spirit. Eleven European football players (all sponsored by adidas, naturally) formed the Impossible Huddle.

The bodies of the footballers represented were 3D-scanned – as were their faces and hairstyles – to ensure that the sculptures were faithful to the originals. It took 40 trucks to move the installation components from the production sites in southern Germany to Switzerland, where they were assembled in the station.

The Swiss rail authority reported that an estimated 13 million people passed through the station during the three-week period the sculptural installation was in situ, and at 17m (55ft) high and approximately 30m (100ft) wide, it was impossible to miss.

Add to this the fact that various news titles such as the *Financial Times*, *Die Welt*, *Gazetta dello Sport*, *Le Parisien*, *NRC Handelsblad*, and the BBC featured the campaign on their front pages or online editions, plus the fact that it was picked up by dozens of blogs worldwide. Who said mass media advertising was dead?

TITLE
SERVIETTE
CLIENT
MCDONALD'S
AGENCY
DDB, STOCKHOLM

CREATIVE DIRECTOR
ANDREAS DAHLQVIST

ART DIRECTORS
**SIMON HIGBY,
TED MELLSTRÖM**

COPYWRITER
MARTIN LUNDGREN

This enormous serviette dispenser – complete
with enormous serviettes – appeared in
Stockholm. But why? To advertise McDonald's
Big 'n' Juicy burger, of course!

TITLE
**OASIS: DIG OUT YOUR SOUL –
IN THE STREETS**
CLIENT
**NYC & COMPANY / WARNER
BROTHERS RECORDS**
AGENCY
**BARTLE BOGLE HEGARTY,
NEW YORK**

To launch and promote Oasis' seventh album, *Dig Out Your Soul*, in the US, the band travelled to New York and taught a selection of street musicians tracks from the album so they could perform them in busking spots around the city.

All of the buskers were taught the songs by the band members themselves and these rehearsals were filmed and hosted online at New York's official tourism site, nycgo.com – where fans could use Google Maps to find the locations and scheduled performance times. The songs were performed all over New York during the two-week period before the official launch date of the album. Fans were encouraged to upload their own video footage of the performances to a dedicated YouTube channel.

A film entitled *Oasis: Dig Out Your Soul – In the Streets*, shot by The Malloys (Emmett and Brendan Malloy) through HSI Productions, documented the whole campaign and was hosted on MySpace. At the time of writing, it had been viewed over 460,000 times.

DIG OUT YOUR SOUL IN THE STREETS

This performance is part of the launch for Oasis' new album "Dig Out Your Soul," that releases October 7th. There are more acts spread out throughout the city playing unreleased Oasis songs today. To find out where these other acts are playing check out the map below.

If you want to upload footage or see this morning's rehearsal with the street musicians and Oasis, please visit www.nycvisit.com/oasis. For more information on the upcoming album visit www.oasisinet.com

① **THOTH 6–8PM**
"Prayformance"
Central Park: Bethesda Terrace

② **THEO EASTWIND 2–4PM**
Singer/Songwriter
Times Square subway —
42 St. and Broadway opposite
Shuttle entrance

③ **PATRICK WOLFF TRIO 3–6PM**
Jazz
Astor Pl. — 6 subway platform

④ **YAZ BAND 4–7PM**
Smooth Jazz
Concourse between E and
6 subways at Lexington Ave.
and 51st st.

⑤ **J. HILL & HARTLING 6–9PM**
Hard Country Blues and Gospel
Penn Station — Long Island Rail
Road subway corridor

⑥ **LUKE RYAN 3–6PM**
Blues Rock
59th St./Columbus Circle A,C,E
subway platform

⑦ **MICHAEL SHULMAN 4–6PM**
Shred Violin
Central Park (at Columbus Circle)

⑧ **GABE CUMMINS 2–4PM**
Jazz Guitar
Grand Central Terminal

⑨ **LUELLEN ABDOO 3–7PM**
Classical Violin
Whitehall St./South Ferry—
Staten Island Ferry Station

⑩ **NEXT TRIBE 2–3PM**
World Hip-Hop/Rock
Penn Station—Long Island
Rail Road Subway Corridor

⑪ **DAGMAR 2 3–6PM**
Art/Performance Rock
Grand Central Shuttle platform

⑫ **MAJESTIC K. FUNK 2–6PM**
Funk
Lexington Ave.–51st 6
subway platform

⑬ **JASON STUART 3–5PM**
Double Bass Rock
Washington Square Park

⑭ **SUKI RAE 2–4PM**
Hard to Describe
Central Park (at Columbus Circle)

⑮ **ELIANO BRAZ 2–5PM**
Brazilian Violin
14th St. A,C,E subway platform

CREATIVE DIRECTORS
KEVIN RODDY, CALLE SJÖNELL, PELLE SJÖNELL

ACCOUNT DIRECTOR
ALEX LUBAR

GROUP ACCOUNT DIRECTORS
CHRIS WOLLEN, SHANE CASTANG

HEAD OF BROADCAST
LISA SETTEN

DIRECTOR OF BUSINESS DEVELOPMENT
BEN SLATER

SENIOR EDITOR
MARK BLOCK

AGENCY PRODUCER
JULIAN KATZ

TITLE
OLIVER KAHN BRIDGE
CLIENT
ADIDAS
AGENCY
TBWA \ BERLIN

If you travelled to Munich for the first game of the FIFA World Cup in 2006, chances are you saw this huge installation, which shows an enormous Oliver Kahn (the then German national team goalkeeper) diving across the motorway.

The 65-m (213-ft) installation managed to bypass the law forbidding advertising on the German Autobahn, and was the only piece of advertising adidas conducted in Germany during the tournament.

Over 4 million people commuted through the installation and many more saw it in the press. In its first week the Oliver Kahn bridge was displayed on double-page spreads in leading magazines including *Focus*, *Stern*, *Autobild* and *Fortune*. It was also picked up by newspapers including the *New York Times* and the *Financial Times*.

CREATIVE DIRECTORS
STEFAN SCHMIDT, KURT-GEORG DIECKERT

ART DIRECTORS
HELGE BLÖCK, BORIS SCHWIEDRZIK

SOAP

TV3

**COLENSO BBDO,
NEW ZEALAND**

To promote the screening of TV drama series
Prison Break on channel TV3, these bars of
soap were placed in public bathrooms all
around New Zealand in January 2008. Upon
washing their hands the user would discover
the impression of a key embedded in the
underside of the soap. This is, apparently, a
common way to make key duplicates in prison.

CREATIVE DIRECTOR
STEVE COCHRAN

ART DIRECTORS
**LISA FEDYSZYN,
JONATHAN MCMAHON**

AGENCY PRODUCER
JO KOUVARIS

ACCOUNT DIRECTOR
KATRINA INGHAM

ACCOUNT MANAGER
LUCY PILKINGTON

CLIENT CONTACT
KRISTEN CARTMER

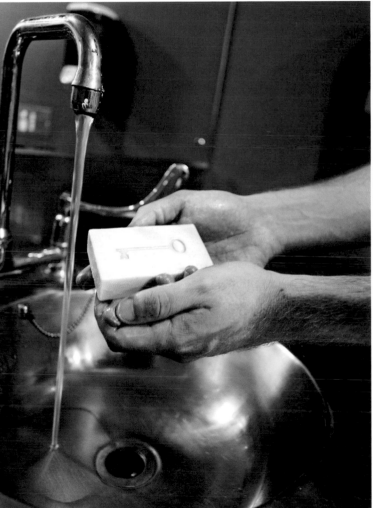

TITLE
UP, UP AND AWAY!
CLIENT
WALT DISNEY STUDIOS MOTION PICTURES INTERNATIONAL
AGENCY
BEATWAX

To help promote Disney Pixar's animated adventure film *Up*, in which a retired balloon salesman sets off on an aerial adventure when he tethers thousands of balloons to his house, UK-based agency Beatwax came up with the idea of creating a hot-air balloon that would look just like the house from the film.

The hot-air balloon incorporated a specially designed envelope, 2,380 cubic m (84,000 cubic ft) in volume, onto which over 500 mini-balloons were singly stitched, so that when inflated the main balloon looked like it was actually a massive cluster of small, colourful helium balloons. To complete the effect, a cold-air house structure was inflated around the basket once the pilot was aboard. The balloon perfectly promoted the film in a host of different locations in the UK, France, Germany and Italy. Media tie-ins were implemented and partners were offered flights in the balloon in exchange for editorial and promotional coverage.

Highlights of the campaign included a flyover and photo shoot at Disneyland Paris, flying into the French premiere of the film in Marseilles, guiding the balloon through the raised arms of Tower Bridge in London, and a publicity stunt at the Leipzinger Platz in the centre of Berlin, right outside the German parliament building, in which the film's director and producer took flight in the balloon. The balloon also appeared in three of the world's biggest hot-air balloon festivals – the Air Balloon Lorraine Mondial Festival, the Bristol Balloon Fiesta and the Warsteiner International Balloon Festival – the combined audiences of which amounted to an estimated 9 million people.

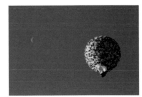

TITLE
THE FUN THEORY: PIANO STAIRCASE / THE WORLD'S DEEPEST BIN

CLIENT
VOLKSWAGEN

AGENCY
DDB, STOCKHOLM

'Take the stairs instead of the escalator or elevator and feel better' is something we often hear, or read in the Sunday papers. Few people actually follow that advice. Could we get more people to take the stairs over the escalator by making it fun to do? This was one of the briefs given to the guys behind The Fun Theory – a website set up as a Volkswagen initiative by DDB, Stockholm. The philosophy behind the site is that people will change their behaviour for the better if they can do so in a way that is simple and fun.

To make the stairway leading out of a Stockholm subway station more appealing than the escalator next to it, the stairs were coloured white and black to resemble a piano keyboard. Each step was fitted with a pressure sensor so that when people put their weight on it, the appropriate piano note sounded. This led to people jumping up and down the stairs trying to play tunes. Much more fun than taking the escalator!

CREATIVE DIRECTOR
ANDREAS DAHLQVIST

ART DIRECTOR
SIMON HIGBY

COPYWRITER
MARTIN LUNDGREN

WEB DIRECTOR
SIMON MOGREN

For another project in this series, the creatives asked themselves if they could get more people to throw rubbish in the bin rather than on the ground – again, by making it a fun thing to do. Their solution was The World's Deepest Bin.

A sensor was placed inside a bin that was labelled 'The World's Deepest Bin'. As rubbish was placed in the bin, the sensor triggered the playback of the sound of something falling for several seconds before a distant, echoing crash, thus creating the illusion that the rubbish was being dropped into a cavernous pit. Footage of the bin on thefuntheory. com shows people enjoying the process of putting rubbish in the bin so much they actually start to look for other objects to throw in the bin.

Each of these installations ran for just one day in Stockholm. But the filmed responses to them are hosted on thefuntheory.com.

MULTI-
FRONTED
ATTACK

We wanted to create something
the fans would embrace and fit in
with Jay-Z's legacy. It had to be
part of his story. When someone
like Jay-Z launches a book it can't
be run of the mill – it needs to be
a pop culture event.

NEIL HEYMANN, DROGA5

TITLE
JAY-Z DECODED
CLIENT
JAY-Z / BING
AGENCY
DROGA5

In October 2010, Droga5's campaign to launch US rapper Jay-Z's book of memoirs, entitled *Decoded*, took the notion of a treasure hunt and implemented it simultaneously in both the real and the digital worlds.

Fans were encouraged, during the month-long duration of the campaign, to find pages of *Decoded*, each of which had been printed and placed in real-world locations relevant to the story/text on each particular page from the book. Traditional advertising sites, such as bus shelters and billboards, were utilized in the campaign, but far more intriguing was the use of some less obvious media.

The lyrics of Jay-Z's track 'Big Pimpin'' – which are about living luxuriously – appeared on the bottom of the pool at Miami's exclusive Delano Hotel, with the content for pages 120–121 appearing printed on beach towels around the pool. Page 40 was printed on wrappers at Black Shack, a burger joint on Lexington Avenue in New York in which Jay-Z once had a cholesterol-fuelled meeting with hip-hop artist Memphis Bleek, and pages 144–145 were located on the stage curtain of the Apollo Theatre in Harlem. Meanwhile, a jukebox in a Lower East Side bar displayed pages 10–11, which deal with Jay-Z's musical influences.

Clues to help people find these pages were released at a rate of between five to ten per day via Jay-Z's Facebook and Twitter pages. And the best way to find a book page was to use Bing maps online via the dedicated campaign website at bing.decodejay-z.com. Once users cracked the clues that guide them to a particular street, a helpful onscreen indicator confirms whether they're getting closer to the page they're looking for, as they move around a location at street level onscreen. However to 'decode' the page, players had to find the page in its real-world location, record the code printed on it, and enter the code online. Any player who located a page online or in person was entered into a draw for a prize: the specific page they had located, signed by Jay-Z. Furthermore, all participants were also eligible for the grand prize: two tickets to see Jay-Z and Coldplay perform in concert in Las Vegas on New Year's Eve. There were over 300 pages to decode before the game finished on November 20, located via 600 real-world placements.

Of course, this isn't just a campaign for Jay-Z's *Decoded* book. 'Bing is a contributing client to this,' explains creative director at Droga5 Neil Heymann of the campaign's tie-in with the Microsoft search engine. 'I'm not sure how widely it's being promoted in the UK, but Bing has had some media push here in the US,' he continues. 'We worked closely with the Microsoft engineers to really make the most of their technology, working directly with their product development team to show off features that are actually still in development.'

But why use Bing at all, was there not a risk of confusion? 'The idea was always to put pages in locations that were relevant to the content,' says Heymann. 'We also wanted to open the game up to people that couldn't be there in person. Bing is the thing that allows people to engage with the campaign online.' Heymann also explains that using Bing's search engine rather than, say, another well-known online search engine, would help players crack clues with a minimum of difficulty. 'Ultimately the clues are being put out to help fans find each page,' he says. 'However, there are some clues where Bing will give you a more direct answer than another search engine. While we were writing the clues we were constantly cross-referencing information with Bing to make sure that it works but actually, in some cases, we're using all their tools. For example, if a clue asks you to study a particular lyric of a Jay-Z track, or look up the number on a jersey in a particular video – then Bing will get you those results in a much more straightforward way than using another search engine would.'

AGENCY
DROGA5, NEW YORK

CLIENT
JAY-Z

CREATIVE CHAIRMAN
DAVID DROGA

CREATIVE DIRECTOR
NEIL HEYMANN

EXECUTIVE CREATIVE
DIRECTOR
DUNCAN MARSHALL, TED
ROYER, NIK STUDZINSKI

COPYWRITER
ADAM NOEL, SPENCER
LAVALLEE

ART DIRECTOR
JON KUBIK

DESIGNER
JON DONAGHY

DIRECTOR OF
PHOTOGRAPHY
PAUL MCGEIVER

SENIOR DIGITAL
DESIGNER
PIPER DARLEY

JUNIOR DIGITAL
DESIGNER
ELIAS HOLTZ

HEAD OF INTEGRATED
PRODUCTION
SALLY-ANN DALE

HEAD OF DIGITAL
OPERATIONS
MIKE JANENSCH

SENIOR DIGITAL
PRODUCER
ANDREW ALLEN

DIGITAL PRODUCER
TOPH BROWN

DIGITAL STRATEGIC
PLANNER
HASHEM BAJWA

USER EXPERIENCE
DESIGNER
CONSUELO RUYBAL

DIRECTOR OF POLYGONS
COLIN LORD

EXECUTIVE OOH
PRODUCER
CLIFF LEWIS

OOH PRODUCER
MEA COLE-TEFKA

OOH COORDINATOR
YAEL BLOOM

HEAD OF PRINT STUDIO
ROB LUGO

STUDIO ARTIST
CHRIS THOMAS

CEO
ANDREW ESSEX

GROUP ACCOUNT
DIRECTOR
SHAWN MACKOFF

ACCOUNT MANAGER
MEGAN COLLINS

ASSISTANT ACCOUNT
MANAGER
LOUISA CRONAN

PHOTOGRAPHER
DAN WELCH, XIAO LI TAN,
FERNANDO SANCHEZ

GENERAL COUNSEL
SCOTT WALDBAUM

VIDEOGRAPHER
SAM KILBRETH

VIDEOGRAPHER/EDITOR
NICK DIVERS

PRODUCTION ASSISTANT
TJ RYAN

COMMUNITY MANAGER
SHALAINA RAMOS

DIRECTOR OF BUSINESS
AFFAIRS
DIANNE RICHTER

BUSINESS AFFAIRS
ASSISTANT
KRISTIN BILELLA

BROADCAST INTERN
BILL BERG

LOCATION SERVICES
MICK BREITENSTEIN

PROOFREADER
CARA MUZIK

EXECUTIVE CREATIVE
DIRECTORS
**PAUL SILBURN, KATE
STANNERS**

ART DIRECTOR
RICK DODDS

COPYWRITER
STEVE HOWELL

PRODUCER
ED SAYERS

MUSIC CONSULTANT
BEN BLEET

PRODUCTION COMPANY
PARTIZAN

DIRECTOR
MICHAEL GRACEY

EDITOR
DIESEL SCHWARZE

POST PRODUCTION
COMPANY
THE MILL

AUDIO POST
PRODUCTION COMPANY
750 MPH

PLANNER
GARETH ELLIS

ACCOUNT HANDLERS
**JAMES GRIFFITHS, SALLY
NICHOLSON, SARAH
GALEA, CELIA WALLACE**

MEDIA BUYING AGENCY
MEDIACOM

MEDIA PLANNER
ANNA BERRY

CLIENT CONTACT
**LYSA HARDY (HEAD
OF BRAND AND
COMMUNICATIONS)**

TITLE
DANCE
CLIENT
T-MOBILE
AGENCY
SAATCHI & SAATCHI

T-Mobile has a strong history of innovation when it comes to product development and customer service, but now with this campaign we're making an even bolder statement about the power of sharing, so everyone knows what T-Mobile uniquely stands for.

LYSA HARDY

Dance was a guerrilla or 'flash mob' event that took place at London's Liverpool Street Station on the morning of January 15, 2009. Dozens of dancers, dressed to blend in with the hundreds of commuters that pass through the busy London train station, performed to a medley of well-known dancefloor fillers played over the station's intercom system, and hidden cameras filmed the activity, which included the spontaneous reactions of the genuine commuters.

The footage was edited, and within 48 hours a three-minute film of the event was aired on Channel 4, filling an entire commercial break during *Celebrity Big Brother*. Following the premiere of the full-length ad, a 60-second version, twinned with ads that included specific T-Mobile product and price-plan information, ran for two weeks. Viewers who saw the advert on TV were invited to press the red button on their remote to view extra footage of the making of the film.

The ad supported T-Mobile's strapline, 'Life's for Sharing' – the idea being that, as a network, T-Mobile allows its customers to share with each other the things in life worth sharing, such as a bizarre outbreak of synchronized dancing in a major train station.

T-Mobile also created a dedicated YouTube channel for users to upload videos and view clips of celebrities being taught how to do the T-Mobile dance by dancer and choreographer Bryony Albert.

'Dance brings to life the fact that there are often unexpected, wonderful, exciting things that happen that you want to be able to share with your friends and family,' comments Lysa Hardy, head of brand and communications at T-Mobile.

TITLE
LET'S COLOUR PROJECT
CLIENT
AKZONOBEL / DULUX
AGENCY
EURO RSCG LONDON

As creatives, we tend to run away from 'real' – it's much more tempting to choose fantasy to make a message more attractive. When we came up with this concept it was clear where its strength was. If we could get something beautiful and poetic out of something real we would have not only an engaging film but a strong evidence of a brand claim, which was always our main objective. And it was reality that made it relevant and easier to explore it in every channel available. The blog, the website, the documentaries and all the content we generated became much more than simply being extra features. They were the campaign in real time and real life from the moment we set foot on the first location. All these layers can't live separately, each part complements the others and is just as important.

FABIO ABRAM, COPYWRITER

Euro RSCG London's Let's Colour campaign for Dulux kicked off in spring 2010 with a TV spot featuring footage of a series of community painting events from around the world, in which people came together to transform dull or tatty spaces into something much more vibrant using Dulux paint or the local equivalent brand.

The first four places to be transformed in this way and which featured in the initial TV spot were in Brazil, France, the UK and India. In the Lapa district of Rio de Janeiro, various homes and a hotel lobby were painted by the Let's Colour team along with dozens of local volunteers. A council estate in Aulnay-sous-bois, a suburb of Paris, also received the Let's Colour treatment. 'Since the 2005 riots this area has been in constant improvement and development, so it was the perfect area to bring some colour to the regeneration project that was already underway,' runs the commentary on the Let's Colour Project website at letscolourproject.com. 'The Let's Colour Project had such an impact that it encouraged the local residents to host their own painting event in addition to ours.'

Virginia Primary School in Tower Hamlets, east London, also features in the TV spot. Together with the parents, teachers and children of the school, the Let's Colour team transformed the school's playground, hall and a classroom with bright colour.

And the fourth of these initial events saw a community square, a school and the main road in Jodhpur, Rajasthan, get a splash of colour – mainly shades of blue, purple and pink.

The TV spot can be viewed on the campaign website – letscolourproject.com – where visitors can also check out the campaign blog, run by Rebecca Campbell of Euro RSCG, which flags up interesting projects from around the world in which colour is a key component, from pieces of artwork to colourful furniture or fabric design and beyond. Viewers can also navigate to the campaign's Flickr page, which contains hundreds of images of colourful homes, streets and other brightly painted objects.

Euro RSCG London is the global HQ for the campaign which, it was initially planned, would roll out in just four territories – the UK, France, China and Brazil. However, due to overwhelmingly positive responses to the campaign, there are at the time of writing 24 markets signed up to experience Let's Colour in one form or another. These include Argentina, Belgium, Canada, Denmark, Hong Kong, Hungary, Ireland, the Netherlands, Poland, Russia, South Africa, Sweden, Taiwan, Turkey and Uruguay – all places where there is a Euro RSCG office and where AkzoNobel (the company that owns the Dulux brand) produces and markets Dulux or a consumer equivalent brand for which the campaign can also function.

The agency is keen to point out that there is no set formula for the campaign, as every market is different and needs to be approached accordingly. 'In some markets it's fine to take the work, such as the TV spot, as it stands, and in others it makes more sense to localize it appropriately – from the websites we build to the print executions we roll out, the social media activity.' Although in most markets the campaign is at a very early stage at the time of writing, more painting events are planned in Turkey, China, South Africa and France. These will, of course, be documented to keep adding to the rich content this campaign is generating.

GLOBAL CREATIVE
DIRECTOR
FERNANDA ROMANO

ART DIRECTOR
BRAULIO KUWABARA

COPYWRITER
FABIO ABRAM

TV PRODUCER
JODIE SIBSON POTTS

DIRECTOR
ADAM BERG

PRODUCTION COMPANY
STINK

PRODUCTION COMPANY
PRODUCER
BEN CROKER

EDITOR
PAUL HARDCASTLE @
TRIM EDITING

POST PRODUCTION
GLASSWORKS

TELECINE
MOVING PICTURE
COMPANY LA

HEAD OF PLANNING
REBECCA MOODY

ACCOUNT DIRECTOR
KEN MULLIGAN,
JESSICA TARPEY

DIGITAL CREATIVE/
CONTENT EDITOR
REBECCA CAMPBELL

DIGITAL ART DIRECTOR
MARIANA COSTA

PROJECT MANAGER
CAROLE SMILA

MUSIC & MUSIC
PUBLISHER
JONSI/UNIVERSAL

CLIENT
AKZONOBEL

GLOBAL CMO
KERRIS BRIGHT

GLOBAL MARKETING
DIRECTOR
LAILA SKIPPER-NORDBY

GLOBAL BRAND
MANAGER
MAREN DUMBUYA

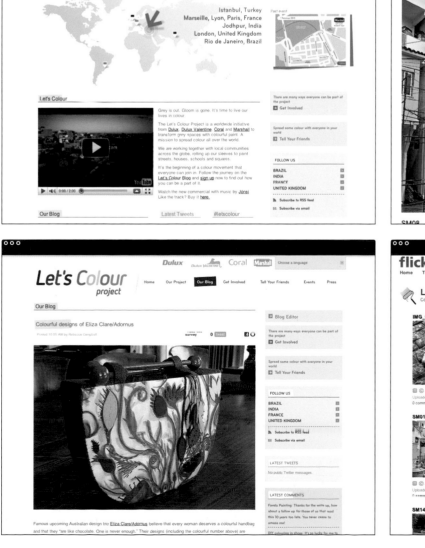

EXECUTIVE CREATIVE
DIRECTORS
ANDY DILALLO,
JAY BENJAMIN

CREATIVES
MICHAEL CANNING,
KIERAN ANTILL, KIERAN
OTS, GARY DAWSON

ARTIST
SHEPARD FAIREY @
STUDIO ONE

DESIGNER
MASATAKA KAWANO

ACCOUNT DIRECTORS
AMANDA QUESTED,
JODI MCLEOD

CLIENT CONTACTS
ANDY RIDLEY, LIZ POTTER

TITLE
EARTH HOUR

CLIENT
WORLD WILDLIFE FUND

AGENCY
**LEO BURNETT,
SYDNEY**

Now an annual event, Earth Hour first took place on March 31, 2007 in Sydney when over 2 million individuals and more than 2,000 businesses switched their lights off for one hour between 7.30 and 8.30pm to take a stand against climate change.

The idea is that the hour of darkness makes people think about energy consumption and how a small action performed by many can make a big difference.

The following year Earth Hour had become a global event with more than 50 million people participating across 35 countries. Global landmarks such as the Sydney Harbour Bridge (pictured opposite lit, as normal, and also in darkness during Earth Hour), the Golden Gate Bridge in San Francisco and Rome's Colosseum stood in darkness for an hour.

Earth Hour 2010 saw 128 countries and territories joining in a global display of solidarity in the face of climate change. Earth Hour has become more than simply a PR stunt, it's developed into an annual social movement of unprecedented proportions.

More details of how to participate in forthcoming Earth Hour events can be found at earthhour.org.

CONTACTS

ACNE ADVERTISING (SWEDEN)
ADVERTISING.ACNE.SE

BARTLE BOGLE HEGARTY, NEW YORK (USA)
WWW.BARTLEBOGLEHEGARTY.COM

BBDO ATLANTA (USA)
WWW.BBDOATL.COM

BBDO GUERRERO / PROXIMITY PHILIPPINES
(THE PHILIPPINES)
WWW.BBDOGUERRERO.COM

BBH (UK)
WWW.BARTLEBOGLEHEGARTY.COM

BEATWAX (UK)
WWW.BEATWAX.COM

BETC EURO RSCG (FRANCE)
WWW.BETC.EURORSCG.FR

BROTHERS AND SISTERS (UK)
WWW.BROTHERSANDSISTERS.CO.UK

COLENSO BBDO (NEW ZEALAND)
WWW.COLENSOBBDO.CO.NZ

CRISPIN PORTER BOGUSKY (USA)
WWW.CPBGROUP.COM/

DDB GERMANY/DÜSSELDORF
WWW.DE.DDB.COM

DDB LONDON (UK)
WWW.DDBUK.COM

DDB STOCKHOLM (SWEDEN)
WWW.DDB.SE

DROGA5 (USA)
WWW.DROGA5.COM

DUVAL GUILLAUME (BRUSSELS)
WWW.DUVALGUILLAUME.COM

ELVIS (UK)
WWW.ELVISCOMMUNICATIONS.COM

EURO RSCG DÜSSELDORF (GERMANY)
WWW.EURORSCG.DE

EURO RSCG UK
WWW.EURORSCG.CO.UK/

FABRICA (ITALY)
WWW.FABRICA.IT

HERE DESIGN (UK)
WWW.HEREDESIGN.CO.UK

JWT SINGAPORE
WWW.JWT.COM/CONTENT/5409/JWT-SINGAPORE

LEO BURNETT LONDON (UK)
WWW.LEOBURNETT.CO.UK

LEO BURNETT SYDNEY (AUSTRALIA)
WWW.LEOBURNETT.COM.AU

LEO BURNETT, FRANKFURT (GERMANY)
WWW.LEOBURNETT.DE

LUNAR BBDO (UK)
WWW.LUNARBBDO.COM

MCBD, NOW KNOWN AS DARE (UK)
WWW.THISISDARE.COM

MCCANN ERICKSON SKOPJE (MACEDONIA)
WWW.MCCANN.COM.MK

METAIO (GERMANY)
WWW.METAIO.COM

MISCHIEF (UK)
WWW.MISCHIEFPR.COM

MOTHER LONDON (UK)
WWW.MOTHERLONDON.COM

OGILVY BEIJING (CHINA)
WWW.OGILVY.COM

OGILVY LONDON (UK)
WWW.OGILVY.CO.UK

OGILVY STOCKHOLM (SWEDEN)
WWW.OGILVY.SE

PERFECT FOOLS (UK, SWEDEN, AMSTERDAM, USA)
WWW.PERFECTFOOLS.COM

PUBLICIS & HAL RINEY (USA)
WWW.HRP.COM

PUBLICIS COMMUNICATIONS, MUMBAI (INDIA)
WWW.PUBLICIS.COM

PUBLICIS MOJO (NEW ZEALAND)
WWW.PUBLICISMOJO.CO.NZ

PUBLICIS MOJO, MELBOURNE (AUSTRALIA)
WWW.PUBLICISMOJO.COM.AU

SAATCHI & SAATCHI LONDON (UK)
WWW.SAATCHI.CO.UK

SAATCHY & SAATCHI, NEW YORK (USA)
WWW.SAATCHINY.COM

SCHOLZ & FRIENDS BERLIN (GERMANY)
WWW.S-F.COM/BERLIN

SERVICEPLAN (GERMANY)
WWW.SERVICEPLAN.DE

SONY MUSIC CREATIVE (UK)
WWW.SONYMUSIC.CO.UK

TBWA\BERLIN (GERMANY)
WWW.TBWA.DE

TBWA\HUNT\LASCARIS JOHANNESBURG
(SOUTH AFRICA)
WWW.TBWA.CO.ZA

TBWA\LONDON (UK)
WWW.TBWA-LONDON.COM

THE BOUNCE AGENCY (USA)
WWW.THEBOUNCEAGENCY.COM

THE PARTNERS (UK)
WWW.THEPARTNERS.CO.UK

TOKYU AGENCY INC. (JAPAN)
WWW.TOKYU-AGC.CO.JP

WIEDEN + KENNEDY LONDON (UK)
WWWWKLONDON.COM

WIRZ/BBDO (SWITZERLAND)
WWW.BBDO.COM/WORLDWIDE

ACKNOWLEDGEMENTS

Thank you to everyone who submitted work for inclusion in this book.

Without their input, support and hard work, this book would not exist – so particular thanks must to the designer of *Guerrilla Advertising 2*, Nathan Gale; my picture researcher Jemma Robinson; and to my research assistant, Ravi Kajla. And also to Clare Double and Jo Lightfoot at Laurence King.

Sincere thanks also to: Eliza Williams, Mark Sinclair, Patrick Burgoyne, Paul Pensom and all at *Creative Review*, Amanda Benfell, Professor Peter and Angela Lucas, Alex Everett, Anna Morne, Ashley Fletcher and Michelle Lockley, Brittany Lippett, Carole Smila, Chris Hilton, Dan Glover, Daniela Mesina, Dave Droga, David Henckel and Jackie Jones, Dominic Goldman, Fred Deakin and Nat Hunter, G$, Gerry O'Boyle, Greg Quinton, Helen Jones, James, Alex and Rudy Joyce, Janice Capewell, Jay-Z, Jeani Rodgers, Jessica Thornley, Jim, Manue et Frida Hilson, Jodi Banfield, Jodie Potts, Joe Wade, Ken Mulligan, Leo & The Waltons, Lien Verbeeck, Lisa Jelliffe, Lori Taylor Arnold, Mark Paton, Maxim and Leo Cackett, Meirion Pritchard, Menno Kluin, Michael Brown, Michael Dorrian, James Sterling and Tony Fox, Mindy Liu, Nat Shah and Rob Jones, Neil Heymann, Peter Glanvill, Phil Clandillon, Roanne Bell, Ru Warner and Vanessa Rubio, and The Peanut Vendors.

Publisher's acknowledgements:

Pages 22–25 NESTLÉ PETERS and FROSTY FRUITS are registered trademarks reproduced with the kind permission of Société des Produits Nestlé S.A., Vevey, Switzerland.

Page 130 The BURGER KING® trademarks and image are used with permission from Burger King Corporation.